COMMON *Threads*

BALANCE

by Dr. Shellie Hipsky

The Missing Piece Publishing

United Kingdom   United States of America

The Missing Piece Publishing

Seathorne Walk

Bridlington

East Yorkshire, YO16 7QP

England

For information visit www.themissingpiecepublishing.com

Book & Cover Design by: Jennifer Insignares: www.yourdesignsbyjen.com

Edited by: Kirsty Holland: www.graceinthesun.com

File Formatted by: Bojan Kratofil

ISBN: 9781-5-136-0423-7

Common Threads: Empowerment

is dedicated to my children and husband...
Alyssa and Jacob,

You are the greatest joy in my life.

You both make your Mommy so incredibly proud.

"Mr. Ken",

I thank God for your support and love.

Thank you to all the amazing people behind the scenes from the "Mommy Army" of transcribers to the fabulous backers through Kickstarter who believed in *Common Threads*. To Neil Haley for being at the beginning of Empowering Women Radio and to all the wonderful ladies who helped with my TV show Inspiring Lives with Dr. Shellie.

To my fabulous Inspiring Lives team especially Brittany Ann Comer, Samantha Barna, Erica Menendez, Christine Marie Scott, Beth Shari, and Chanice Lazarre.

Thank you to the Missing Piece Publishing Team including Jennifer Insignares, Kirsty Holland, and Kate Gardner. To my publicist Jennifer DeCosta from Dash Public Relations for taking Inspiring Lives to the next level.

Thank you to my angel in heaven, Clarel Radicella, for your guidance and friendship. I am "bracing myself" and you were right, it is bigger than I ever imagined.

My family is my world. It began with my loving parents. Thank you Dr. and Mrs. Jack and Libby Jacobs. You gave me the gift of life and then showed me how to make the best out of mine.

My heart is filled with gratitude for the Global Sisterhood of Empowering Women for sharing with Empowering Women Radio your fantastic success secrets.

Thank you also to the amazing woman reading this book right now. It is because of you, that I was driven to manifest this project to empower other women internationally.

Dear Global Sister,

— ♦ —

It has been fabulous meeting empowering women like you from around the world. I can't wait to introduce you to my friends!

In Paris, Kimberly Wilson the author of the *Hip Tranquil Chick* and I indulged in rose petal ice cream after yoga. Lisa Haisha in California welcomed me into her Soul Blazing Sanctuary where she counsels the Hollywood elite; then I traveled back again to her non-profit foundation's glamorous Legends Gala. Cheryl Liew-Chng in Singapore, China chatted with my Empowering Women Radio's audience on thriving as a *24-Hour Woman*. From an award-winning medical doctor who lived in India to a successful business owning mother of seven children who has grandchildren.

The women of the world are seeking answers. Learn from these incredible ladies their ways of making it happen. I love to hear their personal "why" and then "how" they manage it all.

My Global Sisterhood of Empowering Women opened up about how they are able to juggle families and work. I wrote this *Common Threads* trilogy so you could meet them and create your own successful life balancing act.

Hugs,

Dr. Shellie Hipsky

P.S. Make sure you check out my other two books in the Common Threads series. After all... who couldn't use a little extra *Inspiration and Empowerment*?

Table of Contents

Chapter 1: Prioritize 1

  Dr. Hetal Gor 2

  Cheryl Liew-Chng 10

Chapter 2: Self-Awareness 17

  Lisa Haisha 18

  Tiffany Huff 30

  Rea Wilke 33

  Karen Finocchio 37

  Aime Hutton 45

Chapter 3: Explore 50

  Marta Napoleone 51

  Olga Maria 54

  Natalie Bencivenga 61

Chapter 4: Love 65

  Jessica Peterson 66

  Susan Dunhoff 69

  Jess Branas 72

  Valerie Lerch 75

Chapter 5: Wellness and Joy 79

  Dr. Judy Staveley 80

  Rachel Martin 84

Chapter 6: Connections 93

  Demeatria Boccella 94

  Kelly Hadous 99

Beth Caldwell... 103

Erin Bagwell... 106

Chapter 7: Style.. 113

Beth Shari 114

Jackie Capatolla 117

Debi Weiss... 121

NaTasha S. McNeil... 125

Nikole Li Aston 128

Miyoshi Anderson.. 132

Chapter 8: Pay it Forward 138

Rose Morris 139

Jacquelyn Aluotto.. 145

Dr. Roli Chauhan.. 150

Kelly Wallace Ventricle 154

Chapter 9: Family... 157

Dr. Patsy Torres Lucero.. 158

Mani Kamboj.. 166

Jen Forsyth... 171

Alice Beckett-Rumberger 176

Tania Grubbs.. 184

Chapter 10: Serenity 188

Kimberly Wilson 189

Crystal Hayward... 193

Dorit Brauer 198

About the Author: Dr. Shellie Hipsky 203

Chapter 1:

Prioritize

It is a question that has been asked of empowered women throughout history, "How do you balance it all?" Some ladies just shrug it off, a few women in government have justified it and celebrities have even wondered aloud why only women are asked this question.

We are often asked this, because it is a question that has been burning in the back of so many minds. Maybe the question pops into your head when you see a friend on Facebook. She is grinning from ear-to-ear, again. Nary a hair is out of place; juggling her baby on her hip in one picture, running a thriving business, active on multiple non-profit boards and posting fabulous date nights with her happy husband. All you can think is, "How?"

Dr. Hetal Gor:

Women's Own OB/GYN

Dr. Hetal Gor is considered one of the top doctors in New Jersey. She has received awards for her compassion and for her care; she is an amazing gynecologist. Jyoti Soni, from the Global Sisterhood, recommended that Hetal would be the perfect doctor for Empowering Women Radio's discussion on women's issues.

Dr. Hetal Gor explained why she was drawn to the Global Sisterhood of Empowering Women's *Common Threads*. She explained to me, "I saw what you do for women and in general. I was so impressed with your compassion as well. I think we all are trying our best to do the right things for the community and especially for women. I am so proud to be associated with strong, powerful, compassionate women.

"I was born and raised in Bombay in India, and it's a big, cosmopolitan city. I always tell people it's similar to

New York City. It is vibrant. It's amazing. It has the best of everything. I grew up in a well-to-do family. I had different kinds of amenities that most people didn't have. When I was growing up in India, I could see a huge disparity among different economic levels. The differences in the status levels can be very drastic in India.

"We lived in a high-rise, in a very affluent area. We had slums around us. The people from the slum area would come and be our domestic help in the house. I would talk to my domestic help and ask them, 'Do you do this in your house? Do you do this?' I found it amazing that these people were not even thinking about washing their hands or telling their kids to wash their hands, or just basic hygiene.

"So I took it upon myself, when I was a teenager, to go to the slum area and talk to the kids about just washing their hands, or avoiding like, rusted nails and other self-care issues. It felt very rewarding. I thought that maybe I should have a career in the healthcare field because this is what I enjoyed doing.

"I got into medical school and while I was studying medicine, I realized I had compassion for women's issues. I felt very strongly about helping some of the areas in slums, especially in the 'Red Light Districts', as they are called in India, because there is a lot of prostitution in those areas.

"As a medical student, I started going into this area and talking to women about protection, and during this time, HIV/AIDS was really rampant, (it was the late '80s, early '90s), when I went to med school. I used to go out and give them condoms to protect themselves.

"The women were so comfortable telling me about things that they had to go through on an everyday basis; I got very passionate about supporting their needs. I realized that OB/GYN was something that I wanted to do. Not only was it a great thing that I was supporting women but also I could help them with a lot of issues that they were ashamed to talk about with men. It was hard to talk with men about it, because they would talk to them in a very negative way, didn't pay attention, or they weren't sensitive to the needs.

"It's such an incredible thing to deliver a baby and make a woman a mother. I think that it is such a rewarding job that I have. Most often, it's a very happy job when I am working with pregnancy and delivery.

"Also, I am passionate about surgery. I love to do gynecological surgery, taking out tumors and doing hysterectomies. I use minimally invasive techniques through small, keyhole surgeries and I'm very, very good at it. That is why I was honored as one of the top ten gynecological surgeons in New Jersey.

"I met my husband during medical school. We decided to leave India and we went to London. I did my studies in London for two years.

"I am very much a whole personality outside the medical world. I do a lot of nonprofit work. I enjoy culture and events. London was not as fast-paced as I would have thought.

"We came to New York City, I did my training again in OB/GYN, in the Bronx, and I learned a lot. The population was similar to the one that I was used to in Bombay, India.

I enjoyed the whole experience in the United States; so we decided to stay here. Now we are citizens of this great country and that's my journey so far.

"I feel as time is going by, that my practice has matured; I am shifting into cruise control with my daily practice. What we always wanted to do when I was in med school and what made me go into this field, was to help people.

"I definitely enjoy my private practice, taking care of my patients. A lot of people can't afford healthcare. I have noticed that those who don't have health insurance are often small business owners. They are trying to make a living out of their art or passion. Supporting their own small businesses, they can't afford to have insurance. I realized that there has to be something for this population, so I started doing free health fairs as my initiative.

"I got a lot of vendors: the lab which did lab work for my patients, the pharmacy, the physicians and different hospitals that I deliver at and do surgeries. I got everybody involved. I've been doing this now since 2008, annual free health fairs where everybody gets screened for various health issues. "Everyone is welcome at the health fair. We do screenings for sugar, blood pressure and cholesterol. The reason for the morbidity and the mortality is cholesterol, heart attacks and blood pressure.

"I did screenings for women who had heavy periods. They're not eating healthy foods and then they tend to be anemic.

"Depending upon which vendor is available, we also have eye, hearing and optometry screening. We educate about breast exams and gynecological cancers at the free health fair.

"A lot of medical students help with the job fair, which is great because I want them to have passion and empathy. I mentor them on being sensitive and caring to people. You don't go into healthcare just to make money; you have to have the compassion. The theme of helping people must be in you.

"That's my own mission, to help part nonprofits locally and internationally. I give services or lectures; guiding them through education can be a huge step. It's a good karma; it's a good thing. From whatever talent or expertise I have, I am passionate about helping people out.

"I started a medical talk show on TV in English. We answer each and every question about health in very simple terms, rather than using big medical words. I try to explain why putting down the salt is important. It's easy to tell a patient, 'okay, don't eat that, don't eat this,' but it's hard for people to adhere to this daily. I know. I have taste buds, too, but I explain to them why it is important, what can be done to make it taste great without adding to our salt intake.

"Whatever is medically relevant to the community, we talk about on the TV show with specialists. With my 30-minute talks, I reach millions of viewers internationally.

"I write for WebMD, which is a medical literature site, which is our biggest resource when patients are looking online. There is another site called Health Tap; it's a free online site where patients can write a question or get a second opinion, and every night, I write one to two to five responses.

"Dr. Phil's people sent me an e-mail of how many people's lives I've saved and how many thousands of patients took my advice through my responding to questions. I was shocked by the power of helping online.

"So many people can be reached with social media or through the web. I feel that there has been a major impact with the health fair, with my medical talk show, and with my online writing. I think a lot of people recognize that, because I've received so many awards. I've been honored as the most compassionate doctor and the top doc award. The awards are a way of receiving patient feedback.

"I do have a marriage and three children, their ages are 15, 12 and 11. It is definitely a challenging thing but it was more difficult earlier on when they were little. I would work from morning to evening and I would set aside two or three hours just for them; I would give them my quality time.

"When my patients become mothers, they always come up and ask, 'How do you do it?' I assure them that kids want quality time. It is not about quantity. That is where we sometimes get it wrong. I have seen mothers who sometimes stay home and they are miserable. They spent the whole day with the kids, but it is not quality time. They are just physically together.

"I ask, 'How was your day?' 'What do you want to do?' I figure out what interests they have. I find ways to cultivate their interests. We spend time together.

"My daughter loves to bake; I am not a good baker but she is, so I think about what I can add to the kitchen when we bake together. I am a good cleaner so I help to clean up the mess as we go along.

"Now that they are older, we go for walks or swim together. Even if it is just for an hour a day, make sure that you are really there. Be present and attentive. They will remember those moments with you.

My kids are so sweet and they are so sensitive. I think that my kids are learning by example. They see my work ethic; they know that work comes first. So I see that with them, they understand that homework and school comes first. We hardly spend time on TV or the video games. They do have an X-Box and a Wii, but all of those games have an educational component or they are interactive.

"We love music. My children are all learning an instrument and to sing. They are learning Indian and American culture. I like to do activities around that to empower them to be their own people and be well rounded. We spend time doing constructive, rather than destructive activities.

"I juggle a lot at night. My best solo work hours are from 11pm to 2am depending on how busy my next day is going to be. I write emails and articles; I update my medical knowledge with medical journals. At the same time, I am doing laundry, I have a pot cooking for food for the next morning, and I am always doing more than one thing at the same time. This becomes a big time-saver for me.

"I do very little (fortunately or unfortunately) in the way of pampering things just for me. I don't go for two-hour massages or manicures/pedicures. I prefer to use that time to use that time to make someone else's life happy. If I can do something positive every day to impact another person, I feel so grateful.

"I teach medical students how to have a career, as well as a family. I have many students who have taken up OB/GYN as a career and they write to me, and say, 'they would not have even thought about it until they saw how my life is with my practice, my kids and all the other things that I do like singing and dance.' Since they see that I can do it, they feel that they can do it as well.

"My message for the Global Sisterhood is to 'be true to you. Be true to your character. Be a person who does what they say they are going to do and make their dreams happen.'

"People will see it. Yes, there could be jealousy and negativity for others because others can't do what you do. Understand where they are coming from. Don't sink to their level. Find the positive in every situation and person. You can balance your life in a positive way."

Cheryl Liew-Chng:

The 24 Hour Woman

Cheryl Liew-Chng is the powerhouse author of the bestselling book, *The 24 Hour Woman*, who lives in Singapore. We talked about her recent book launch, "Oh, it was fabulous. We went straight up the charts on Amazon. It's a wonderful thing to see. The women who are getting the book and joining our Facebook group discussion are fascinating. There are lots of interesting conversations going on about *The 24 Hour Woman*.

"The whole concept is that we all have 24 hours in a day. What do we do with our time, energy and our very presence, and what does the 24 Hour Woman do, given that we are torn in so many directions, in our various roles?

"We are daughters to somebody. We are moms possibly to somebody, a wife or a friend to somebody, a team member and a leader.

"So what is 'the 24 Hour Woman' to do? Are we really fulfilling our own legacy at the end of the day? We need to really feel the life balance. We should be proclaiming, 'What an awesome day I had today'. That's what 'the 24 Hour Woman' is all about.

"I run my life-training program around the world. It is still evolving and I am refining it. I'm a good mom first. My husband and I, we are raising three boys, so that, to me, is number one. I am raising three young men that are responsible, that are God-fearing; they are contributing to and leading their community.

"Secondly, it is important that I'm a good sister and daughter. I have only one sister, and we are very close-knit family; so for me, family is important.

"The work that I do and the life I live have directly impacted and made a difference in the lives of others. Those in my life, live a life that is worth living with boldness, courage and passion.

"I say, that without my husband, all of this would not have been possible. Without him, I would say that my legacy wouldn't have been possible." We discussed how there are a lot of men out there who are very important in their wives', girlfriends', or mothers' lives and supporting them.

Cheryl said, "I would say that that's absolutely true, and I think over a long period of time, these supportive male partners advance women in corporate and entrepreneurship. It is so positive to be among male champions and support.

"There's no better time than now for 'the 24 Hour Woman' to really, pause and rethink… What do they want their lives to stand for? What is their legacy? How can they build their legacy on a day-to-day basis?

"Some legacy stems from parenting. My three boys are 8, 12 and 18, so that's a huge age gap. My husband is always joking that, we are watching 'Finding Nemo' again and again, but I think raising the boys in this modern time is no different from, say, my parent's generation. Even though, with the Internet and all, there are a lot of distractions.

"There are a lot of things that we can't prevent, yes, but I would say that in the good old days, there were a lot of things that our parents could not have prevented either. However, technology and just the pace of change have made it more challenging. Raising children, given that they do learn a lot more, and are exposed to a lot more than we were, is tricky.

"I think the fundamentals of parenting build a firm foundation when we go back to them. Get back to listening. Value your children as individuals. Give them a voice and impart values when they are young and then just guide them along when they become a teenager.

"My eighteen-year-old is now a young man, and guiding, as opposed to asking him questions in terms of his own decision-making, has always been the way that my husband and I raise our boys. We are very thankful that they are growing up into fine, young men. That is what we can do as parents.

"We know that as they're growing up, we probably will not be there all the time for them in school, or when they're traveling. Fortunately, it is my belief that my God will look after them wherever they are. In fact, he's probably doing a better job than I am as a parent."

It was during this interview with Cheryl out of Singapore, through Skype that during the break my real mom life was revealed. I uttered on Empowering Women Radio, "Cheryl, I will admit something to you, I'm trying to do this radio show and my little son just curled up on my lap. He really did, and he's looking up at me with these big, brown eyes and he's supposed to be in bed, so I too, am a '24 Hour Woman'. That's for darn sure! I need some tips here, Cheryl, so do the other women in the world. What can we do to balance it all?"

Cheryl replied, "Yeah. That happens to me when I have my 8-year-old, when he's not adhering to his schedule. We all are '24 Hour Women'. We all have 24 hours, so what do we do at the end of the day, and if, at the end of the day, you can tell yourself, 'I'm fulfilled.' 'I'm happy', and I can tell myself what an awesome day I've had, then kudos. That's a great job, no matter how you have made it happen.

"So many of the women that I have worked with, through our training program or our live events, they come to us and they say, 'I'm so disappointed, and I'm just so tired at the end of the day. I don't feel a sense of fulfillment or vibrancy. I really don't know what to do.' I do not wish this feeling for anybody.

"It is true that there's a lot on our plate, but I think as I've written in the book, *The 24 Hour Woman*, it is about navigating this season in our lives by being smart and by living with our authentic selves. Turning away things that are really 'not who we are' and are just 'other people's expectation of us'.

"I do spend a great bit of my time working from home, and I've since learned to set up a routine. I hang something at the door when I'm working and I tell them, 'Mom is at work,' and then at a certain time, I'll come out and I'm totally at play with them. So the one little key piece is about being present and into whatever you're doing, so the children feel that you have given them your time and your quality attention.

"They are happy that you did spend time with them, rather than being distracted. They know that you really care and love them.

"I also have to say no sometimes to my girlfriends. They complain, 'I haven't seen you in ages, Cheryl. You've been so busy writing your book,' but the book was important to this season in my life. I've learned so many things in my personal life about navigating life's challenges about thriving in our work and business, and yet, living a vibrant life.

"I wanted to share what I learned; to be able to share the stories of the other women who have been successful in using what I teach them. So for me, it was saying no to my social calendar for a season and then connecting back in again right now with my friends. I do say that there are certain things that I will say yes to.

"I will say yes to family routine; I will say yes to things that are important to the family.

"I will say yes to my girlfriends sometimes, because there are five of us that have grown together; we challenge one another. We support one another, both personal and professional development, and I think that's important, because as a '24 Hour Woman', you need to be able to create your own support system. Sometimes being strategically able to say 'no' means having one of them delegated to follow up on your behalf.

"I wanted to just funnel all that learning down to the '24 Hour Woman' book, sharing the five pillars of the 24 Hour Woman: how to build the support system and become a woman of impact and influence." Cheryl spoke directly to me when she said, "Because at the end of the day, each of us is a '24 Hour Woman' is a woman of impact and influence, just like you are now to your cutie pie that's on your lap; that he is really looking at what you're doing, and modeling your ways."

She explained 'The 24 Hour Woman Mastery Program'; "It helps readers to move from the book to having an experience. We guide them through a six-week program, because we know that transformation doesn't take place by you just reading. You need to be doing. Sometimes, in the doing part, you need a coach, or you need somebody to just go with you on your journey.

"If you visit "the24hourwomanmastery.com", they have the whole training CD, and I also have a program called 'The 24 Hour Women mastery online program'. We also do live events where the whole room is filled with dynamic and significant women. When you come, you are a part of the community. You bring the experience and friendship back with you to support your '24 Hour Woman lifestyle'."

Chapter 2:

Self-Awareness

Who are you? I spent my teenage years trying on different personality types, like most girls try on shoes. With each reincarnation of myself, there was a new wardrobe, different ways of interacting, a unique friend group and more. There was the "hippie-chick" version who did a very brief summer tour with the Grateful Dead band. The punk rock version with my repurposed black clothing from Goodwill, black lipstick and large safety pins through my ears. Even into my adult years, I continued to reinvent myself time-and-time again. My friends have said that I have had more lives than a cat.

Lisa Haisha:

SoulBlazing Institute and Whispers from Children's Hearts

I sat with "Soul Blazer" Lisa Haisha in her beautiful home in Sherman Oaks, California. The surroundings in her sacred home were beautiful. Everywhere my eyes landed, were visual representations of stories of her travels internationally. There was a huge map of the world with millions of little pins in it, with pictures and images attached. I couldn't wait to share Lisa with the Global Sisterhood.

Lisa explained why she was drawn to this special space, "I needed to be in Los Angeles. I started in Hollywood, because that's what you do when you move to LA. Then I slowly started finding my way around. Then when you get married, you leave the west side and you go over the hill, where the studios are. You know, my husband is a television producer, so it's ten minutes from the studio. I was a writer; I work with people as a life coach, and they come to me, so it's like we moved to where my work is."

Lisa explained what Soul Blazing is, "It is a type of therapy that I developed after working with so many people, hundreds of people, and I was basically just talking through their problems. I was giving them their homework to do; providing them with things to think about. I noticed it wasn't working that well.

"When I went to a prison to go work, it was four days with a group of people. A really tough prisoner challenged me saying, 'Okay, do your thing. I've been in prison for twenty years; nothing you do is going to change me.' Then I said, 'twenty years?' She said, 'yes;' she was a lifer and she was the bully of the prisoners. I said, 'Okay, I'm going to do something different with you, then. Let's experiment.'

"I started having her improvise. I taught this imposter concept that I came up with, because the ego was huge. When I talk to people they say, 'Oh, it's your ego or ego does this, or ego does that.'

"They get it, but they don't get it. It's kind of like having a baby. You get, 'Oh, I have nieces and nephews. I get what it is to be a mom.' Then when you're a mom, you're like, 'Oh, my God, I got it, but I didn't get it, because you're not living it every day.'

"I cut the ego up in eight pieces. I named the egos as your 'sex god/goddess', 'narcissist', 'wounded inner-child', 'over-thinker', the 'counselor', and three other labels. I exposed all these different facets of who we are and figured out which one leads each person after seeing them in so many people I was working with.

"I told this prisoner, 'You're a narcissist and you need to get your way, and you killed because of this, and this and this,' and then she started crying and opened up to me. After about 30 minutes of our session, this tough prisoner said, 'Lisa, you just blazed my soul.' That moment is when I exclaimed, 'You just gave me the name for what I do. I'm going to call myself a Soul Blazer!'

"It was an emotional moment. The woman in prison began our connection exclaiming, 'Who are you? You're some, white chick, who has lived this kind of life, and you have no idea what it's like to grow up in, Brooklyn with no money and poverty. You don't know the craziness and homelessness.'

"Yet, once I related to her on her level, she got it. As we started doing experiential exercises, she got it even more. So I started doing that with clients, so it's really like a master improvisation class and having fun with your own issues. I don't actually coach you. I coach your imposter; I teach your imposter to make a deal with you to make your life easier.

"I have them take an imposter quiz, so it's sort of cheating. They can come in saying 'this is who I am,' and then I work with them. Their king or queen imposter is the one that they know; that is who they are. I think the most interesting people have a lot of imposters. All the great artists or musicians have lots of imposters. We're all nuts.

"I think I have five or six out of the eight. I'm like oh, my God. I shouldn't even be teaching this, I'm so messed up. I look at the imposters, and all of our icky sides, but even our icky sides could be positive if they're coached the right way.

"I look at imposters as a pit bull. So many people are afraid of pit bulls, and, 'Oh, they're scary, they're dangerous.' Even if you train a pit bull, (one of my friends just got one) and I was like, 'No, I don't want to come over with my six year old. I'm scared. Even if you say, 'she's a sweetheart'; maybe she's going to have that one moment with my kid.'

"After my friend assured me that it was alright if I went over there, it was the sweetest dog ever. It's like if you train your pit bull to be nice from when it's a baby, it could be a wonderful loving pet, but if you don't train it, it could bite you or bite someone else and really sabotage your life. That's like your imposters.

"If you train your narcissist, you could have your narcissist work for you when you need it, but if it just goes off, then it's going to mess up your life. If it's going to be the bully at work, being the arrogant one or stepping on anyone to get to the top… then you might self-destruct. You may be rich, but you won't be happy.

"It comes down to taming them. If you use your sex god or goddess to get what you want, then you're going to have worries of, 'I did this; I had that, and who knows the drama that's going to play out?' It might get what you want for a year, and then it's going to fall apart. If you use it when you're on a date or with your lover, then it works out great. It's better if you are not using sex as a weapon or as a tool, but use it for the right reasons."

Because Lisa stated that you could be rich, but not be happy; I asked her what success is to her; she said, "Oh, my God. That's such a great question, because it can have so many answers, but to me, success is being happy. It's having mind, body and spirit all connected. When you wake up every morning giggling and laughing; meanwhile, the whole world could be falling apart around you, but you still find the blessing in the moment."

Lisa's dream vacation is coming up soon. She explained, "I'm going to go visit the Dalai Lama. I am staying in palaces and spending two days learning from him with a group of ten or twenty people there. My husband bought it for me at an auction, so all the money goes to the children of India. We have a charity, 'Whispers from Children's Hearts'. It's a nonprofit, so we're giving it through that company.

"'Whispers' is something that organically came about. When I was a teenager, my dad got mad at me. He was born in Iraq and we lived in San Diego. He had five girls, all within a year apart. He felt that if one got out of line, all of us would, so he was very strict. We weren't allowed to date, or do other typical teenage girl things.

"So one day, he came home early, which he never does (because he always worked 8:00am until 11:00pm). I was just baking cake three houses down at my girlfriend's house, for another one of our friends. I came home in my school uniform, my Catholic school uniform, blue and green checkered, and my knee socks and my Wallaby shoes. He threw a fit.

"He was asking what I was doing. Saying that the streetlights were on outside. I was like, 'I'm just down the street; mom knew.' He said, 'No, this can't be happening while I'm at work. Who knows what else is happening? Send her to an orphanage…' and he told my mom, 'Call an orphanage.'

"My mom said, 'We don't have orphanages.' He demanded, 'Call one anyway! Find someplace to put her!' There was lots of drama and crying; I went to my room and slammed the door.

"Years later when I was 27, I was going through a mid-life crisis. I was here in LA acting, but I couldn't take any role because I couldn't do nudity; I couldn't simulate nudity. I got a B movie, and I couldn't even like whisper in a guy's ear; my dad was always in the back of my mind. If the director wanted me to wear a see through shirt, I couldn't do that. I decided to quit after a year and a half.

"Someone said that the way to be good at anything is to know who you are. I realized that I didn't know who I was. I was always asking others what they thought about my life. To discover myself, I went to Iraq alone. It was when President Clinton was bombing, so nobody else would go with me.

"I went to at New York International heading to Jordan, then I took an 18-hour bus ride to Iraq because they didn't have any airplanes flying into Iraq because of the bombing. I met a woman there who was sitting there by herself. I said, 'Where's your family?' She said, 'Oh, I'm here by myself.' I said, 'Oh, going to Jordan?' She replied, 'No, Iraq.' I'm like, 'What, are you nuts?', and she stated, 'No, I want to go kill myself.' I thought this was great. I exclaimed, 'Oh, my God. Really? Me too!' It was kind of a strange bonding moment.

"I was totally going through this life crisis; I didn't know what I was doing, so we started laughing and chatting. We decided that we would just go together. It was very exciting, so we got on the plane.

"We both didn't want to be together at the same time, because we both really wanted to be solo. Our problem was that we both love people so we surrounded ourselves constantly. We're never alone, so when you're never alone, you never have time to think and reflect. Both of us wanted to go to Iraq. She was born there; she moved from there when she was four.

"I wasn't born there. I wanted to see where my dad grew up. I wanted to see an orphanage there, so we both were 'kind of' tentative at first getting on the plane. We said, 'Oh, just keep your seat, I'll keep mine,' but then when we got to Jordan, it was a three-hour layover there and then the eighteen-hour bus ride.

"Several times, the guys pulled us over like the cops, and they came in and searched the bus. We were told that those guys sometimes rob you or kidnap you. So we were both in the back trying to make light of the situation saying, 'Hello, don't forget us, hello,' and it was really funny. Then we ended up becoming very close friends, best friends.

"Unfortunately, she just passed seven months ago. We were going to go to Barcelona together. That was always on our bucket list to go live there for a year, and that's why when she died in July, I left in August for Barcelona."

As the author of *Common Threads*, I'm finding so much with this Global Sisterhood that's being created; that women can form these amazing bonds so quickly, and it's like instantaneous when you have that common thread or that link to each other, it is beautiful."

Lisa explained what happened when they arrived in Iraq, "There's this place, Mosul, kind of where Saddam Hussein was from. We went to Telkaif and Mosul, which is where all the Caledonian Christians are, and that's what I was, a Christian Iraqi.

"Then we went to where my friend was born. She lived in a cave there. So we went to her cave and the only other things in that area were a small little hospital, an ice cream truck, a church and a little grocery store.

"We found an orphanage. I started talking to the kids. The kids were saying, 'Why are you talking to us? Nobody cares about us. Nobody loves us.' I was like, 'We do. We do,' and they said, 'Nobody cares.'

"I got an idea and I said to the children in the orphanage, 'Talk and I'll memorialize your words.' So I started asking three questions, and then the answers were so deep and so profound. I continued to do that, and did 15 countries after that. I wrote a book about it, and then from that, I started bringing supplies and stuff to these orphanages. *Whispers from Children's Hearts*, my book with the words of the kids, just happened."

Since Lisa wrote *Whispers from Children's Hearts*, based on children's answers to just three questions, I posed those same questions to Lisa. I asked the first question from the book, 'If you had one wish, what would it be, Lisa?' Lisa grinned at me as we were taping for Empowering Women Radio and said with a smirk, "World peace." She was messing with me of course by giving the pageant pat answer. She settled into her couch and continued on a more serious note, that her one wish would be, "It would be that every person, especially women, would find their voice."

Lisa then responded to the question regarding whether or not God is fair. Lisa surprised me a bit when she responded, "This is a tricky one for me, because I don't really believe in God, but most of the world does, so I included that question in my book for the children. I believe in the universe. God is in my heart. God is in my soul. I believe God is my authentic soul, and so nature is God. Evolution is God. So, yes, I think it's fair, you know, because we all evolve, but what happens in the world is I think everyone's own doing. I don't think God is up there as a puppeteer telling each of us what to do, creating good guys and bad guys.

"I think if you have faith and you believe in yourself, you can develop yourself. I don't think it works on just having faith alone. I believe you have to empower yourself; you have to bring out the passion through your heart, which I think is God. Through that faith, you have to have discipline, and really learn the tools. Get a life coach or create a game plan yourself to get what you want and stick to it.

"Nothing is created without action. I think your thoughts create your reality, and if you pray and just focus healing or praying for someone else, it's helping them; It can give them a peaceful send-off, like my friend who was passing, everyone was praying for her to live. She didn't live, but I think it helped her to feel cocooned in love. We gave her a positive mindset to transition to wherever we go when we die."

The final question that she asked the children in her book could certainly be posed to anyone. I asked Lisa Haisha, "Who in the world would you most want to meet?" She responded, "It has been the Dalai Lama, and I'm going to get to meet him, and if it wasn't the Dalai Lama, I think I would want to meet the Clintons. I think they have done so much positive in the world, even though they've both been raked through the coals. I do think they both have good hearts and want to do their best in the world, so I would really love to have a sit-down with them, meetings of the mind, and I would love to be part of the global initiative and do something on that level.

"I have workshops and retreats continuously, so if you want to go to Lisahaisha.com or the soulblazinginstitute. com, all the information is there; I am now offering soul-blazing certifications, so you can become a soul blazer. If you're a life coach, you can tag that onto your expertise, or we teach life coaching and then you can apply to become a Soul Blazer."

Before I left her peaceful home in Sherman Oaks, California, I noticed a string of colorful beads. I asked Lisa about the beads and she told me, "I got them from a woman in Nepal when I was traveling there. They're special to me because she was special. She had just a beautiful soul. She loved my earrings.

"They were gold, Egyptian, like prayer earrings, and she was just so fascinated with them. She was like 90 years old and almost toothless. Her wrinkled hands kept grabbing my earrings. I was like, 'Here, take them." She was like, 'No way. They're yours,' and she went and got me that bracelet so that it was a fair trade."

I became so passionate about Lisa Haisha's work and mission to connect the people of the world who help children, that I traveled to back to California for her Legacy Series Gala. I was blown away by her friends including ladies from the Global Sisterhood featured in this trilogy (author Pina DeRosa and actress Brianna Brown) and other socially-conscious celebrities such as Deepak Chopra's daughter Mallika Chopra who founded Intent.com a social media company that helps establish work-life balance.

Yet, the moment at the Legacy Series Gala that brought the crowd to our feet was when they played a video from the hit TV show the X Factor. The footage featured a talent and handsome vocalist who did not have fully-formed arms or legs due to surviving chemical warfare. Emmanuel Kelly and his brother were adopted from an Iraqi orphanage by an Australian woman who has helped thousands of children in need. The video showed his story and announced that on the TV show, he would be singing.

The screen faded to black… and into the red carpet gala came Emmanuel Kelly singing Imagine by John Lennon. This was days after the Paris terrorist attacks in 2015 and many of us were still reeling and praying for peace. The tears fell down my face as I stood together with leaders from multiple communities soaking in the lyrics and being present in the moment. Lisa Haisha's dream of inspiring the leaders of movements internationally is certainly coming true.

Tiffany Huff:

The Best You

I love both Tiffany's spirit and her freckles. She has created 'The Best You' and 'When She Thrives' organizations with the mission of leading courageous women to step out on faith and live in purpose, on purpose.

Tiffany explains in her journey in her own words, "I was bankrupt, and not only financially. I was emotionally, mentally and spiritually empty because I had given so much of myself up for others that I had nothing left.

"I was abused. I was shot by the love of my life, the father of my children; but, I was also abusing myself because I refused to give myself the love and care that I needed.

"I was homeless. I was shot during the tumultuous end to the relationship and had to live in a domestic violence shelter out of fear. At that point, I was so out of touch with who I was at my core, that the real me had no place to go.

"I am creating a community, a safe space for the single mothers who feel the world has forgotten about them, so they know that God hasn't. It's a place where you will be challenged to use your adversities, your voice, your pen and acts of love; break the chains of all the reasons the world says you should just survive and begin to build a legacy in which you, your family and community will thrive.

"My name is Tiffany Huff and I'm the head mom on a mission, and founder of 'When She Thrives'. I believe that you are enough and that you deserve to 'simply break free' to be free. Free to be who you were called to be, to create what you were chosen to create and to build the legacy that you were purposed to build."

Tiffany and I talked about the problem of labels such as "homeless" and "bankrupt"; she stated, "I think that often those labels do set a standard, and we can be guilty of taking on the roles that those labels define, even if they aren't actually who we are. I know that part of my journey was being able to shed those labels. I had to become who I am, unattached to those labels, by removing them. That is very hard to do, assimilated to the labeled, and assumed those responsibilities. That's why I often say that it takes courage to be the best you, because removing those labels can be scary.

"You have to get uncomfortable to become comfortable again. Once you decide that you're not going to assume those roles defined by those stereotypes, you're going to begin to be set apart.

"Initially, it can be uncomfortable. It's like walking into a room and everybody has on black and white and you show up in red, so everybody is looking at you; but once you become comfortable and recognize that you like red and you feel good in red, then it's okay."

Tiffany also started a program called Sisterhood Speed-dating so that women can find each other quickly, get to know each other and form meaningful friendships and mentoring relationships. Tiffany explained, "It's one thing for us to sit at home or write in our journals or even dream about the person that we are becoming or want to become. It is another thing to speak life into that person, and that is what sisterhood speed dating is all about."

The questions that we ask each other during these sisterhood match-ups aren't as straightforward as you would think. They elicit some chuckles. They will make you think. They encourage you to inspire other women and be inspired as well.

One of the questions during Sisterhood Speed Dating is, 'What is your super power?' We get to know each other, learn about our goals and objectives for life. We support and build each other up towards our dreams. Rip off the labels and embrace your own dreams.

Rea Wilke:

Your Life Now

Rea Wilke is the New Jersey-based CEO of 'Your Life Now, LLC', and an executive coach. She explained her business, "We focus on people who are really looking to make positive changes in their lives. They are hungry to live a better life, whether it's on a personal level or a professional level. We provide professional coaching and training, leadership training, as well as marketing solutions for our clients.

"Coaches really have to think about their clients' needs. This goes back to my sales training and the philosophy of NLP, which stands for neuro-linguistic programming.

"It's about the other person; so when you are a coach, you are a mentor. You are somebody who is a teacher, a guide. We have the saying, 'When the student is ready, the teacher appears.'

"The teacher is the coach. I see myself as a teacher. I get to know that person that's seeking help and see what it is that they need to bring awareness to. I don't think anybody needs to be fixed. Coaching just brings the awareness that we all have something within us that is a lot more powerful than what we think. We can pretty much have control over our lives at any level if we know that. A good coach brings awareness, knowledge and shows the steps to achieve what they want in life.

"Neuro-linguistic programming is literally, what it sounds like. It has to do with the language of the mind and also your physiology as well. It is how you speak, what you say, what you say to yourself, what you say to others and how you express yourself physically. Our body language is also a language, so the combination between the two, makes the person who they are.

"In neuro-linguistic teaching, we bring awareness to our words. Words have a lot of power. You can uplift somebody with words; you can put somebody really, really down with words. We all experience it. I have experienced it, where somebody has said something to you and it hurts, right, and it's like, 'Oh, my God. I can't believe that person said that to me,' because the words have so much influence on you. The teaching of language encourages proper word choices.

"For example, a person shouldn't say, 'I don't want to fail,' because what comes after 'I don't' is 'fail,' so your mind cannot distinguish between the two; so all your subconscious mind hears is 'fail'. Therefore, you should say, 'I would rather succeed' or 'I would like to learn how to succeed' or anything pertaining to what it is that you really truly want with the positive end result.

"So what do you want? You want to succeed, right? You don't want to fail, so that means you would like to succeed. Just choose the proper words.

"It's really just as simple as practicing it as a skill. We've all heard before, 'Practice makes us perfect.' Repetition works.

"It is your physiology and it's your neurology, which are a mind and a body connection. Then you also have your environment, right? So we all react to things or we act on things.

"When you are reacting, you're impulsive. You're not thinking about it. It is the first thing that comes out; most of the time, we pick the wrong words.

"I get very excited talking about this topic, because it's really important for us to realize and understand what we say and how powerful those words are, then we choose them and change the outcome by tweaking them.

"If you don't know exactly what's going on in your mind and how you're feeling, just ask yourself. Stop and ask, 'How am I feeling right now?'

"Just by doing that, you're bringing yourself back to this moment. You realize that, 'I don't feel comfortable being surrounded by that many people; so I'm feeling anxious.' That anxiety is expressed in your body, too. You're not only, giving a verbal reaction to how you're feeling on the inside. Your body is showing it as well, and people can see through that.

"Women, ask yourself what matters to you first. Set yourself a priority list. Get to know what your skills and talents are. Know where you can improve, and set yourself to be different from that next person next to you.

"A vision is not just a picture of what could be. It's a call to become something more. Bring that to your awareness. That little extra can give you an edge, in a society where competition is so prevalent.

"Don't worry about the rest. We get so worried about like, 'Oh, let's see who else is doing what I'm doing,' and I don't know if I can compete with them. You don't need to be in competition.

"Have an open mind and an open heart. Question everything. Live your life your way. Stay present. Take chances in life. Breathe and smile. You are alive. You are amazing."

Karen Finocchio:

One Tough Muther®

Karen is spunky, strong and an amazing mother of four, who went through a rough divorce. She knows what it is like to rebuild and then thrive. Karen described how we connected through social media, "I remember reading something you wrote online, Dr. Shellie. It was on Facebook to someone we were mutually friends with; I thought that your words were very kind, but at the same time, a bit soul searching.

"I sent you a friend request and when you accepted, we immediately clicked. You and I were going through some parallel issues in our personal lives. I felt your struggle to sort it all out, because I too was challenged with that, a similar situation.

"I thought it would be great to send you a 'One Tough Muther shirt'. I was sending them to women who needed just a little more strength, a lift and a nudge to get them through a rough patch in their lives. I loved that you proudly wore your 'One Tough Mother' tank top.

"I have sent out almost $5,000 in inventory to women all over the world. These beautiful women internationally write me back or send me a message. They say that wearing the shirt gave them power, made them feel in control, stronger and more confident to face their personal issues. I loved hearing it so I continued to offer them to women in need of that power. Actually, I still do this. I sent three out yesterday!

"I started 'One Tough Muther' ® on the advice of my adult children. Everywhere we went people would seek me out and ask me questions. Whether it was the grocery store, the beach, a function or an event, someone would come up to me and ask me for help with something. They would start to talk to me and tell me their problems or ask my advice on an issue they were having.

"Being a single mother for a large part of my children's lives, living in so many different places, and learning so much from my experiences or other people's experiences seemed to give me a treasure trove of wisdom to share with others.

"I remember my youngest, my daughter saying to me, 'Why do people always come up to you and ask you for help?' My answer was, "I guess I just have a face that others think they can trust." My son actually said once, 'Mom you should write an advice column and call it, One Tough Muther, because you really are.'

"I do many podcasts and radio interviews. The responses that I get from the women who hear them are just unbelievable.

"I went through it. I was a single Mom. I was in an abusive relationship. I have struggled to feed my family and on and on. Women say they find it easy to identify with me because I speak to them like a friend or a sister, even when I have never even met them.

"My vast amount of real life experience seems to touch so many women with every interview. I am just overwhelmed by their love, honesty and the way they open up to me.

"Speaking to women's groups and young women for that matter has become a passion for me. It has taught me so much. I have learned more about myself in the last two years than I learned in my previous 50 years. I am super excited to say I am currently mentoring with a fabulous woman who is preparing me to become a women's motivational speaker.

"I have realized that all the trials, troubles and tough times I have gone through have prepared me for this next adventure in my life. Now I will help other women learn strength, confidence and true self-worth.

"The last two years have taught me that my passion is my true purpose for being here on this earth. When you find your passion, your purpose will surely expose itself to you. All you have to do is accept it and let it live and grow within you.

"My favorite advice column response is very tough to single out. I really love speaking to young women in their 20's and 30's who have grown up in a time where their mothers had to work. They didn't get the one-on-one attention of a mother being there when they may have truly needed it.

"I have always said that your children most definitely need you when they are babies, to teach them, guide them and protect them. However, your teenagers need you as much or more, because the teen years are scary, dangerous and extremely confusing.

"My children who are now in their 20's and 30's were pushed to talk to me. Was that always the right approach? Probably not, and did it always avoid troubled times in their lives? Certainly not; however, it did give them a base, some structure, a sense of love and protection as they tried very hard to navigate the teen years of discovery and hormones.

"Every woman has something valuable to offer someone in this ever-changing world. A few words or a helping hand, a hug or an understanding ear; that of another woman, may be just what is needed of to get through a rough part of their life.

"I was fortunate to learn and work with all the major New York radio stations, placing ad buys, writing and voicing commercials, being a guest on the shows, including the Howard Stern Show.

"I spent a season with Ozzy and Sharon Osbourne promoting products through Ozzfest. I adore Sharon; she is a very kind, caring and smart lady.

"I have worked with MTV's "Jersey Shore kids", History Channel's "Pawn Stars" and cast members of HBO's "The Sopranos". I've recently met and spent time with Wendy Williams, at her studio, during her show and continue to develop and plan large media campaigns. I spend a great deal of time in New York, Los Angeles, Las Vegas and Miami with my creative friends, top level producers and network connections where I flourish and continue to grow.

"While my career was growing, my personal life was a roller coaster ride. I've lived through one life threatening marriage and one life saving yet painful divorce, lost my biggest fan and supporter, my father, and was present when someone I loved committed suicide. I did everything with only a high school diploma.

"I was blessed with four smart, funny, kind and awesome children, which I am extremely proud of and have been hands down my absolutely biggest accomplishment in life. Each of them had their share of growing pains and it was tough, but we are family in every sense of the word, forever and always. I have been blessed with my purest joy, which are my five beautiful grandchildren. We always support one another; even if we don't always get along or agree on something, we hold ourselves together with love.

"When people read all the things I have done in my life, hear my interviews or see my bio, they ask, 'How did you learn to do so many things and work with so many interesting people?' The answer is easy. It all happened because someone else reached out their hand to help me. I have had such a vast amount of life experience thanks to my Earth Angels (as I call them) saying, 'Hey! Let me show you. Let me teach you. Let me help you.' I have been so very blessed to get as far as I have. It is due to the help of so many wonderful people willing to teach me, guide me and help me.

"Then there are the Angels we don't see that are always with us, giving us choices, direction and guidance. Those Angels are within you. You just have to believe. Believe in your own heart, character and soul. You have to be willing to say 'I believe I can do anything and nothing anyone says will stop me, because the only person who can ever really stop me is me.'

"Life is about learning and learning is about trying. You can only fail at something if you never try. Failure is an event, not who you are.

"When I was asked to do something, even if I knew nothing about it, I would try to figure out how to do it. I use to tell my kids, 'I may not be the smartest person in the world; however, I am smart enough to find some way or someone to teach me what I need to know and to learn from there.'

"The secret to my success is… this life, this story, this adventure was never really about me. Yes, the good and the bad happened to me; I was the character written into this plan; yes, the choices I made led me to the place I am now; however, this story was really all about you. It's my purpose. The reason I was placed here, the direction I was given, the lessons I learned were to help you, and others like you.

"All roads that you follow in life can lead you through the good and the bad. You have to fight for what you want. Believe in who you are. You have to break, pull yourself together and break again, over and over until you realize that life takes courage and heart. You and only you must define who you are and never give that power to anyone else. Success and happiness doesn't just come to you, you have to make it happen.

"The only one who is ultimately responsible is you. It is the choices you make and the way you allow those choices to affect you.

"Fear is just a word, it is something you make up in your mind that you give power to. Danger is very real but fear is not.

"You must learn to believe in yourself the same way you believe in others. If I can do it, you can do it… all you have to do is believe.

"Ask for help, look to learn, take baby steps every day until one day, your stride changes and you begin to run. Learn that we are our happiest when we are making others around us happy.

"Find your passion and you'll know your purpose, and once you know what your purpose is, you are unstoppable. All roads lead to one place in the end. Live your life, for it is truly yours to live.

"I let my pain, the times that dropped me to my knees… push me farther. You can do the same because we are all equal, flesh and blood. Do not allow yourself to be a victim.

"Stand strong and empower other women, because, Baby, the times; they are changing. This is our time to show we are powerful. In closing, I will quote a woman whose courage and character I admired, Elizabeth Edwards, 'She stood in the storm and when the wind did not blow her way she adjusted her sails.' Ladies, adjust your sails!"

Aime Hutton:

Inch-by-Inch Empowerment

Aime Hutton is an International Best Selling Author from Canada who empowers teen and tween girls. Aime Hutton explained to Empowering Women Radio how her mission got its start, "It started when I was looking at some of the struggles from my own life. Many of these challenges came when I was between 4th and 8th grade, which is your young tween, early teenager age group. I was severely teased and bullied for 6 years. I didn't believe in myself. I thought I was the names I was being called like 'stupid', 'ugly', 'retarded' and a loser. So I know where a lot of those girls are right now today and how they are feeling.

"I developed *Inch by Inch Empowerment* (with both a teen and a tween girl component), to target ideas about being themselves. It is about being brave and your authentic self. For the older girls: I go into dating violence, body image and stress. We discuss juggling time management for everything between school, homework, my job, extra-curricular activities and my family and friends. These hot topics for this age group are all discussed in the online-program.

"In recent years, I've gifted my program to girls in Kenya, and they absolutely loved it. I got feedback a few times from them; one of them actually wrote back to me saying 'I'm sitting in my village in our council meetings and my voice is being heard because I'm speaking my mind. You gave me the courage and confidence to do that'. The adult contact I have in Kenya, wrote to me and he said, 'Aime, you've changed and saved my girls' lives.'

"There are three main things that I talk about when I'm in live sessions as well: just put one foot in front of another, believe in yourself, and let others help you. Letting others help is really important. I know that I feel I can do it all by myself. It's the pride in myself that makes me not want to feel vulnerable and ask for help.

"I'm involved with the e-Woman Network, which is the largest North American networking group for women in business and entrepreneurs. When I first joined the group here in Calgary, our chapter's managing director at the time, Jo Dibblee looked at me and said, 'I want to help you grow and glow. I want to help you.' I had never been told that before. Jo said, 'You know what? You're going to do this and I'm putting you on stage at an event. You are going to do what you do!'

"At the event that I spoke at, the businesswomen really got in touch with their fun and feminine sides, dancing around and strutting their stuff. We all had a good time feeling confident in our bodies. I love to add feathers and sparkles to glam up the participants so the ladies can experience having fun being bold.

"I work with young girls as well. Being bold is all about being yourself and not being afraid to step outside your box. I tell them, 'It's ok if you want to read books and play Dungeons and Dragons and go on the computer and design games. That's cool; if that's what you want to do, do it fully. If you want to go into music or the arts, do it fully. If you want to, go into politics, go for it.' They can do whatever they feel they want to do, if they put their mind to it.

"The first book I compiled, which became a best seller in six and a half hours on Amazon, is called *Inch by Inch, Growing in Life*. This has 30 stories, written by adults, who overcame adversity before they were 12 years old.

"My reason for the book came when I was sitting in the children's hospital around the beginning of November, and I saw a poster for World Premature Birth Day. That was literally my sign, because I was born in 1976, I was 3 months early and my birth weight was 1lb 12 oz. I was given 24 hours to live.

"I thought to myself, children overcome adversity; why not put a book together about that? So, I gathered people from around the world, Canada, United States and one lady from Scotland. We all shared stories about, for example, medical miracles, like a premature birth, medical trauma, overcoming child abuse, and living with disabilities. These were about different social stigmas that were all happening to children under the age of 12, and how they all overcame them.

"Some of the stories in this book are remarkable! What I like to say too is, 'If these children overcame what they did when they were under the age of 12, then you as an adult can do anything!'

"It's also a book to help heal families and children. I've chosen to donate one third of the proceeds from Amazon back to the Children's Hospital of Eastern Ontario in Ottawa, Canada, that saved my life. My mission is to give hope to families who are sitting in the hospital right now, that have just been told their child is not going to live. I can't speak as a parent, but what I can say though is 'know that this journey in the NICU is going to be a roller-coaster'. You're going to go through highs and lows; just take it one hour at a time and just celebrate all the tiny little accomplishments.

"Ladies, let yourself just dance and play. Take some time for yourself. Engage in self-care and be gentle with yourself. I know every woman in the world has umpteen million things going, but if you can't look after yourself, how are you going to look after others?

"So, take the time and put on one piece of music. Find a song you like, play it and just dance. Tell your husband or your partner that 'I am taking three minutes to be by myself'. Also, tell your children that 'Mummy loves you; I just need three minutes'.

"Lock yourself in the bedroom and play that piece of music and just dance and give yourself a hug. If tears or emotions come up, know that's ok. Just breathe and dance through it, because you want to be the choreographer in your own dance of life. You don't want to be sitting on the sidelines, in the wings. Be that dancer in the spotlight in your own dance of life."

Chapter 3:

Explore

Turning my graduate students' attention towards the ceiling, we all glanced towards the glory of the Sistine Chapel. I was blessed to have the opportunity to teach future teachers in a summer semester in Rome, Italy for Duquesne University.

Travels calls to me; New experiences, unique people, fantastic cultures and of course the delicious food. I dive into it exploring, to discover myself as much as to learn about the places.

Marta Napoleone:

Marta on the Move

I enjoyed being interviewed by my dear friend Marta Napoleone in her home studio for her podcast 'Marta on the Move'. Her lifestyle has always intrigued me. I enjoy listening to her travel stories and learning about the people she has met along the way.

Marta told Empowering Women Radio about the first time she traveled to a foreign country to volunteer and learn, "This project in Sicily was a tomb excavation, and I was blown away. They were taking volunteers; you just paid for like room and board, and it just seemed so crazy to be out there.

"I immediately dialed Italy and hadn't even thought of the time change. I woke some poor, little old lady up. I felt terrible, and I couldn't speak Italian very well, actually at all. I just had a little bit of background. She didn't speak a lick of English, but made it through, and I completed a wire transfer of funds that very next day.

"I had never done that before. I felt like a spy. The bank people looked at me like I was nuts, and booked my ticket, and did it all within two days. I was petrified because I didn't ask anyone to go with me. I didn't even ask my mom, you know, if I could go, even though I was still living under her roof at the time."

She continued her exploration of the world through unique adventures, "I started looking at France and the South of France. They were restoring a tenth century castle in this little town called Saint Victor la-Coste, about 40 kilometers away from Avignon. Once again, I went for like three weeks on that one, and it blew my mind.

"Recently, I went on a marine study of dolphins and whales in Italy. We got to actually live on a boat and learn how to navigate the boat. We learned how to tie all the knots and help out the wildlife, in Italy, off the coast of Ishka, so that was really cool."

I inquired as to what she has learned from all of her adventures internationally, "I didn't have to conform to everybody else's viewpoint of me. I could be myself, and as long as you are yourself, you are in control. That's the only way to live your life. That's really the most important thing that I learned.

"I also learned that being afraid of something is not always a bad thing. If something is scary because it's outside of your world of comfort, it's usually a good thing. It's almost like you are on the right path if you're scared of it. Most people don't want to do that. They veer away from that. They just want to stay in their comfort zone, so that was a very important thing for me to discover about myself, that I could reach beyond my limitations even though I was scared of something and just go for it."

She talked about her lovely family (including her fabulous sister who is also my friend, Nina), "I think the most important thing is to help each other. It can't be a competition. Just really appreciate the person that you grew up with and the person that will always support you. Try to remain close."

Marta reminds us that we should strive to simplify our lives. "We don't need to have as many things. Recognize that you don't need that expensive car or an expensive TV. What you need is the experience. You need to get rid of some of your stuff, really. It's not the size of the house you have; it's how much stuff you put in the house. It's more about the memory than the object."

Marta urges you to, "Please travel. Please travel alone. On my site, I had five tips for why you should travel solo abroad, at least once in your life. I just urge people to do it so much, especially women, to get out there and experience life because after all, there's only one of them. You only have one shot. You want to take in all of it while you can.

"I promise you will come back with the best stories and the best moments of your life. Also, you'll take something from yourself; you will discover more about yourself interacting with these different cultures. Do it, just cut the cord of comfort. That is really what I would love to tell women out there, more so than anything else."

Olga Maria:

Dreams in Heels and Ladies Travel Pass

Olga Maria is a dynamic and beautiful fashionista with a heart for charitable giving and travel. She explained how we met and a bit about our friendship. "Dr. Shellie Hipsky and I met online when she reached out to me on Facebook to attend New York Fashion Week. At that point of my life, I was doing PR for different fashion designers and beauty lines. I had my own public relations company called Dreams in Heels.

"Dr. Shellie and her 'Inspiring Lives' team, were given media passes to attend the different shows when she came to New York. At the Waldorf Astoria Hotel, they taped the pilot for her TV show and recorded what was happening behind the scenes. It was a magical time. I love how Dr. Shellie supports other women's dreams. I really admire her so much, and we became good friends.

"I remember when Dr. Shellie flew me to Pittsburgh to stay for a few days. I was treated like royalty. She and her team took me to do hair, makeup and to film her Inspiring Lives with Dr. Shellie show at the NBC studios.

"A few years after, Dr. Shellie and I kicked off our businesses in NYC with a fantastic VIP party for a great cause. The night was benefitting Beating Cancer in Heels, an important non-profit organization. I organized the fashion shows' aspect, silent auction and more. It was a powerful evening with women entrepreneurs."

Olga explained a turning point in her life, "I was 18 years old when I came to New York from my island of Puerto Rico; even though in Puerto Rico they teach some English in school, I didn't speak it, write it, nor did I understand it. I read it a little. After a year, I acclimated myself to the American lifestyle and I learned English by immersing myself totally in the language. I had to struggle a lot, working many jobs, renting rooms, until eventually I was able to start going to college.

"I won't deny that many times even though I was born in NY, since my mom took me to Puerto Rico at 6 months old where I was raised, I felt like an immigrant because I didn't speak the language. Nowadays, I'm a travel, fashion and lifestyle writer for different publications and I'm also the founder and editor-in-chief of the blog-a-zine, *Dreams in Heels*. Some of my work has been published on the *NY Daily News*, *Vetta Magazine*, *Livid Magazine*, an *Expedia* travel guide and more. My travel writing excursions have led me to Asia, Europe, Latin America, the Caribbean, across the United States and Canada.

"When people meet me and hear my strong Latina accent, they ask me if my articles are in Spanish, but no, they are all in English. I have come a long way; I would like to encourage other women to follow their dreams. Just don't stop, life is too short. If you believe, everything is possible.

"I decided to create Dreams in Heels to inspire other women to live a more adventurous life, to follow their dreams, to travel more, enjoy the journey; all the while, doing it in style! 'Dreams in Heels' is your passport to travel and dream in style!

"Where did the name come from? Well, I'm always in high heels. I always travel, and walk around in heels. Some people ask me how I can walk in heels all day. Well, many don't know this, but I have a condition in my legs. I was born with a shortened Achilles' tendon. When I was a kid, children bullied me because I couldn't walk flat. I always walked like a ballerina from a ballet. They also bullied me because I had natural curly hair. The truth is that the bullying I dealt with as a child, made me stronger and I started following my dreams in heels. I had to overcome all my fears, all those kids mocking me... in heels.

"Heels are for me are part of my lifestyle and I want to inspire other women to follow their dreams; it doesn't matter what condition they were born with, what race, what religion, we are all unique. If you were not born like that, you wouldn't be the woman you are today. I was born this way, and I wouldn't change one thing. I just embrace it every day with a smile. I'm truly blessed!"

I asked her what her favorite travel memory is and Olga replied, "I have so many amazing travel memories. I'm always jet setting off to every corner of the globe in heels. Switzerland was incredible because I felt like I was in four countries at once. I experienced the Swiss, German, French and Italian cultures in Switzerland. I went from Zurich, to Bern, Lausanne (French region) and finally to Lugano (Italian region). It was amazing! I loved the culture, the people, the food, local wine, fashion/style, the stunning views, and the fresh air. Even the water was tasty! It was a unique experience.

"I also can say being in China and climbing the Great Wall in heels was a highlight from my travels! I'm always living up to my mantra, 'Living my dreams in heels.' I visited 5 cities in china: Beijing, Xi'an, Nanjing, Suzhou and Shanghai. When I meet Chinese people, some tell me that I know more about China that they do. Honestly, I really fell in love with the gardens, the history, culture, food and shopping. China was a truly lovely experience.

"It's interesting to see the excitement of the people when they meet you. Simply cause you look exotic to them. They want to take a picture with you, talk to you, and they smile. I even got some senior citizens take me out to dance in the Lake Park in Nanjing. It was wonderful to see how we didn't speak the same language, but body language was everything.

"Your life wasn't meant to be lived in one place; it's like staying all your life on the same chapter of a book. There is so much to discover out there so turn the page!

"After all my traveling, I noticed how many women still wish to travel, but most were either afraid to travel on their own or their friends' schedules did not match them. Sometimes, their friends did not have the same resources to travel as they did.

"I feel that everyone should have the opportunity to make their dreams come true, travel more, live better, experience unique activities and connect with new people from all over the world. For this reason, I just created a new company, Ladies Travel Pass. Ladies Travel Pass enables groups of women to travel safely in style and comfort.

"Ladies can meet new people, experience new cultures and indulge in unique activities. We can check out the nightlife, get pampered, eat well and shop! Group travel for women not only connects us... but it helps us to better understand ourselves, and the world around us.

"Ladies Travel Pass creates a non-competitive environment of support, encouragement and sisterhood. Our trips are all about immersion of new and enlightening cultures all while being true to yourself.

"I have met so many amazing women on my adventures that have inspired me. One of them is Anje Collins, the owner of Luxe Public Relations group and author of *PR Related*. She is one of my mentors. Anje is a very strong woman that fights daily for the rights of women in PR. She creates workshops, resources and she has inspired so many in the public relations world. Nobody could tell that Anje struggles daily with cancer.

"Another woman I met on my path has been Ena Jordan, who is part of the academic affairs staff at the community college where I first attended. She has been my mentor over the years. She helped me with my English vocabulary, my writing skills and even with my career path at the beginning. She's one of the angels of my life.

"I can't forget to mention, a person I met after, in my path while I was doing my bachelors at Baruch College and working at Hunter College, Denise Lucena-Jerez. Denise is a powerful and kind woman who has followed me on my adventures. She is the person who proofreads and edits all my work and encouraged me to write for publications. Denise always told me, 'You can learn grammar, but never perspective. The way you see things is just amazing.'

"I feel everyone needs mentors. I encourage every woman to find a mentor and advisor. Also lifestyle coaches are great to help you find your purpose and follow it.

"An empowered woman is someone who finds their purpose and follows their heart and dreams. She wakes up every day with a strong desire, a real passion and does what she loves. She never feels like she's working, cause she's following her dreams. Nothing will stop this woman, only God. She's driven, determined and full of energy. She loves adding value on other people's life, helping and encouraging others. Most importantly, she doesn't compete against other women cause she knows that everyone brings a different flavor to the plate. Everyone is unique on their own way. So why be jealous? As women we can help each other and succeed together!

"I invite women of the world to be the best version of herself. Be present now. Be open to new possibilities and be true to yourself. For me, it's not just about the destination, but the journey is just as important. I encourage you to go out to explore, wander, and expand your views. Discover every day a little bit more about yourself and about the world (and all of its happenings) around you. "Above all, do not fear making mistakes or dealing with life's little changes. Never let anyone else write your story. In return, for good karma, always lend a helping hand. A little action can cause wonders.

"Last, but not least, follow your dreams and find your purpose. Nothing is more rewarding or valuable than having a powerful reason to wake up every morning. Life is your canvas; start painting today! Follow my journey as I keep 'Living my dreams in heels.' Remember that 'Mi casa es tu casa.' Expand your horizons and stay fashionable."

Natalie Bencivenga:

Pittsburgh Post-Gazette SEEN and Ask Natalie

"Natalie went from a social worker to a journalist at fabulous events. She explained her journey, "I had always been a writer and I co-founded a healthy living and relationships webzine, which I ran for five years. In that time, I was doing a lot of media work and decided to go back and get some letters after my name to solidify my 'relationship expert' status. I went to the University of Pittsburgh for my Master's in Social Work in 2011 and I have my license.

"I was working as a mobile therapist at the same time as running my webzine, which I ended in 2013. I was approached by a colleague just a few weeks later, who told me that the SEEN columnist at the Pittsburgh Post-Gazette was retiring, and that I should apply for the job. The rest is history!

"As an advice columnist for a major paper, there are pressures to get the responses right; because of my therapy background, I take everyone's questions very seriously. I try to respond as thoughtfully as I can (in such a short amount of space!). Oftentimes, I email the person back directly with a much longer response, because I want them to know that their question was important and that they matter. Sometimes we get into email exchanges if they have more questions, which I love.

"I really like to respond to the questions that focus on the pressures of being a woman. I get a lot of questions from young women about body image and pregnancy. One in particular was a question about bodily autonomy, and how uncomfortable a woman (who was pregnant) felt when people would touch her stomach without permission; she was afraid to speak up for herself, fearing how she would be perceived. I suggested that she put her hand on her stomach and say that she is feeling 'extra' protective of her space, because she is pregnant.

"I don't believe others can empower us. We have to empower ourselves, but we can guide to that place of self-love.

"Sometimes the biggest risk is to take no risk at all. I am a firm believer in the fact that it is better to make a mistake than to stand still out of fear. If someone is ready to make a life change (big or small), they need to decide how this will impact them (most importantly), the others in their lives that they love and if it is going to be helpful or harmful in the long run, but I always tell everyone, 'Listen to your gut.' You know what to do. Believe it.

"Both my younger brother and sister are very important to me. We were all very close growing up and I love to see the wonderful, hard-working and loving people they have become. Having a sister eight years younger than me has always been very special because we have never been competitive like some sisters are. We are incredibly supportive of one another; I try to always support my brother and sister and let them know that no matter what they are facing, we will figure out a solution together.

"I love how easy it is to connect to family, friends and the world through social media. Email, Facebook, Twitter, Instagram, Snapchat...the list goes on and on and on; it's easy to connect with readers and also to keep up with the pulse of what is happening in the world.

"But, the problem with social media is that it is all superficial. It is a great way to open a door, but that's, as far as it will take you. You have to be willing to take the next step in networking and meet someone face to face to really learn about them, to determine how you can be effective for one another. Also, social media flies past us all day long, and how can you absorb everything? You can't, and that's okay.

"I want to speak to the ladies out there reading *Common Threads*… We are the new leaders. We will be the ones to change this world for the better. Women have a unique perspective on things that has not been tapped into and fully appreciated.

"Ours is a collective experience, a global connection. We are masters of communication, masters of networking. We think in a pragmatic sense and these are the skills leaders need in today's world.

"We must lift one another up. Support each other and recognize that a victory for one is a victory for us all. Remember to compete only with yourself and collaborate with all around you."

Chapter 4:

Love

Love can burn an ulcer in your stomach. It can tear your heart out. But when it is mutual, reciprocal and healthy... it can be the profoundly beautiful thing that nurtures and uplifts you as you join souls.

Jessica Peterson:

Customer WOW Project and Purpose Powered People

"What I love about your show, Dr. Shellie, is that you keep it real. It wasn't scripted; I didn't know what you were going to ask. The only thing you told me is we're going to end with an inspirational minute right at the start of the show.

"I really am seeing a lot of women struggling in knowing who they are and their purpose and their mission. My wish is for every woman to know who they are, their purpose and their mission, and then to collaborate with other people and to move ahead in full force.

"I was actually talking to a woman today. Ironically, she said, 'My heart wasn't really feeling full, and I knew I wasn't living my full calling, and I was in reflection mode on who I am and my purpose. I said a prayer and then there you were.' She said, 'You're literally an answer to the prayer.' It was so kind. After talking, she says she knows her purpose and her meaning. She feels she can run with it. That makes me so happy. That's my wish for every woman, to know their purpose and their passion and to run with it."

If you don't know what your purpose or passion is, step back and think about as a kid what you loved to do. This can often lead to recall how you are at our core.

"When my husband lost his passion and his purpose, he was in a funk, and it was a hard journey. Other women have come forward saying they're in that journey or they're watching their husband go through it, and it breaks my heart because I've been there. My husband is always happy and positive; then we went and volunteered in Belize for 28 days, which was one of the best experiences of my life. We did whatever our heart led us to do. We fed people, gave people hope, helped a girl get married, and there's just tons of stories there.

"However, when we got back, everybody was telling my husband what he should and shouldn't do. My husband is all sitting there thinking, 'Okay, why are you getting upset?' So, I said, 'Forget everybody. What just makes you so happy? And just what do you love, just anything?' And he looked at me, and said, 'Something with gold, maybe gold mining, and helping people, and I don't know how to combine it.' I didn't verbalize it, but I was thinking, 'Oh, I'm going to have to move to the mountains. I'm a city girl.' You know, and I just looked at him like okay. I said, 'At least we're at a start. We're finally at a start.'

"It was maybe two days later, a friend of ours, who is a former cop, sheriff and successful businessman came to my husband and I; we've known this very successful, caring gentleman for over ten years. We hadn't heard from him in a while, and he shocked us by saying, 'Hey, I'm doing something with gold and helping people.' My husband had actually verbalized what he wanted and his next opportunity came to us.

"Don't give up; it's going to take time to start anything, and you really have to have faith in yourself and move forward, and also I think any new business really needs to get out there. You can't just sit back and expect that things are going to come to you.

"One of the biggest, most important things I did was really networking and getting myself out into the area. I met new people. I am always talking to people about my business and I think that's so important because word of mouth nowadays is really important. Being able to get your name recognized is essential in a new business."

"Selling is really all about educating people, taking an interest, caring for them, and supporting other amazing people. Whether we do business together, that's great, and if not, that's fine. That's okay. We've still got to support each other. I've had people who say, 'Wow, you still want to support me even though we're not working together?' I said, 'Yeah, that's what it's all about. It's just supporting good people, and, you know, moving ahead in this world, even if we do work together or solo.'" You can make a profound difference in your lives and in others by giving without asking for anything in return.

Susan Dunhoff:

The Modern Matchmaker Inc.

Susan Dunhoff, Professional Matchmaker and Relationship Expert started The Modern Matchmaker business in 1991. She met her husband-to-be, David through her matchmaking firm and married him over 20 years ago. Susan has a BA in Journalism and MA in Communications from Duquesne University, and previously owned a successful marketing communications firm.

Susan is skilled in getting on a client's wavelength quickly and figures out what they want in a perfect match. She only recommends compatible people and makes quality introductions so they do not waste their time.

All of her clients can get a date, but have come to The Modern Matchmaker to find the right date. They are selective and want a committed relationship.

Susan explained, "Our female clients; are all busy professionals, and they say, 'I don't need a man to complete me. I have a wonderful life.' They just want that void in that one part of their life to be fulfilled, and it should be someone that complements them, not completes them. They're complete. It should enhance their life or it's not the right person.

"You don't want a clone of yourself because it's boring. Sometimes if you're a little bit on the shy side, an extrovert pulls you out; at times, a little bit of an opposite personality works.

"I would say quite a few of our clients know what they're looking for, or think they know what they're looking for, but not always; we help them figure that out. It could be, age; It could be family and children. It depends, because we match up from ages 25 to 85, so it depends on what stage of life you're in to determine what's important to you as well. It's the whole picture: education, interests, height and physical character.

"A lot of our gentlemen say intelligence is a turn on. They want a confident woman. They don't want a needy, clingy woman; they want someone who is emotionally stable. Financially stable helps as well, of course, it doesn't hurt!"

Susan discussed how it can be very empowering for women to meet that right life mate or partner. She said, "It's a wonderful thing. It's almost magical when it works. When you are matched with a really good significant other. Even when you are falling in love, it may be three months into a relationship, whatever it is. It enhances all aspects of your life. You work better, you're happier. You know someone cares."

Jess Branas:

LesBe Real Radio

Jess described our long lasting friendship, "I met Dr. Shellie about 15 years ago when she started coming out to the Havana dance club for salsa nights. Shellie is quite the dancer.

"She clearly had so much passion and joy for life. It was infectious and rubbed off on all of us. As she became a part of our salsa family, she brought something with her. She brought inclusion and support.

"At first, our 'family' was small, but loving. Susie Rudolph, Irasema Fatter, Amanda McKee Chamberlain, Char Barnett, Kristen Licht and I were some of the original tight tribe that tore up the dance floor.

"Not only did Shellie light up a room when she walked in, but was always eager to join in and bring people together. As the years went on, she included each and every one of us in her ventures and has supported us in all of ours.

"This in itself established our incredible salsa family. Having a family outside of your blood relatives is important for women to have; not only for fun times, but support and love through all the good and bad.

"I am one of the on-air radio personalities for the LesBe Real show. LesBe Real Radio is an outlet for the discussion of issues within the LGBT community, as well as providing entertaining perspectives on relevant LGBT news. Whether it is hosting a youth initiative or covering major community milestone events, LesBe Real focuses on bringing the communities together.

"I was fortunate to have a very loving and supportive family. They raised me to be gracious, motivated and strong; so I didn't have too many struggles while I was growing up.

"Although I did have some relationship struggles in adulthood, each person that entered into my life taught me a little bit more about myself. The end of a long-term relationship was what started me on my journey. Without that and the other relationships, I wouldn't have become an author and dating coach. More importantly, I wouldn't have realized the true meaning of forgiveness and how resilient a person can be.

"However, my biggest personal struggle was going through thyroid cancer about three years ago. This is what truly shaped me. I finally understood the importance of putting oneself first and believing that one can overcome any obstacle. It strengthened my love for family, and determination to stay present and joyful every minute of every day.

"For a woman to find and sustain love, she really needs to know herself, what she wants in this life and her expectations of herself and others. Hopefully, women will take the journey to discover all the greatness they behold and show that to the world. If you are looking for a partner, you must be accountable for all the energy you allow into your life, so you can make the right choices for you. But in reality, it's not about finding another person, it's about finding and sustaining the love you have for yourself.

"Women are the great organizers of the world. It seems as if many are 'Superwomen' that can handle it all. Every one of us has the power to achieve anything that we dream, and yes, it does take a lot of determination.

"On the other hand, it also takes the ability to stay present in the process, and finding time to keep yourself healthy and balanced. When you juggle kids, careers, goals and all other aspects of life, taking the time to breathe and be grateful works wonders on one's stamina.

"I want every woman in the world to believe in and take care of herself. Give yourself permission to laugh and love. Enjoy everything life has to offer. Feel desire and dream. No matter what this crazy world can throw at us, and long as we support each other and say 'yes' to ourselves… everything is possible!"

Valerie Lerch:

Posh Events by Valerie

Valerie Lerch's company, Posh Events by Valerie, helped to bring the Fabulous Forties Gala to fruition; combining fantastic fashions from the 1940's with food and live entertainment, raising money for the Homeless Children's Education Fund. Valerie credits connecting with other professionals, with her ability to juggle her event planning business, motherhood and being a counselor for children during her day job.

Many times, I have seen Valerie at her events surrounded by people who care. I caught up with her at one of her events and she said, "I am very blessed to have an extremely supportive family. My mother is actually on her way now to help out. She was watching my kids this morning, which is a blessing."

We talked about people she looked up to, and her mother instantly popped into her mind. She said, "My mother, was a teacher and she was very much into running events and helping with our church and other charitable organizations. She was in the Business Professional Women's Club for many years, so I saw her doing that. I really enjoyed helping her with it. My organizational skills are really helpful in event planning. That's what I love to do.

"Of course, there is my amazing husband Micah, who is a huge part of my life and has been so supportive of all of this. I'm driving everybody crazy sometimes with all the work and everything I have to do, but he's always there for me. Even looking back at the Fabulous '40s, my husband just jumped into action; in fact, we had a little glitch there where we needed someone to go usher people into the VIP dinner and my husband just took it on, and he did a great job. I'm very blessed.

"I really think I got lucky, I do. I think love is one of those things that just happens. But, I believe you have to have similar goals. I also think sometimes opposites attract because we don't necessarily share all the same things, so I think that was part of it, too. We kind of balance each other out well."

Her husband, Micah Lerch spoke with me at the business expo that Valerie had coordinated. He jokingly said, "Behind every empowered woman is a tough man who does what he's told."

Valerie explained her business that garners support from her awesome family, "The Posh Events brand brings parties and conferences that are classy, high energy and really also help provide funds and needed things to non-profit and charity organizations. Branding is really important; one of the things that I decided to do when I first started this business was to make sure that I was identifying who my customers were, because looking at these type of events, you might think that the customers are the customers actually coming through and buying products. However, my customers are my vendors, because they're the ones that I want to make happy. I want them to come back, do well at the show and be successful. I think that is part of helping empower other women."

Other than her mother, Valerie was so kind to say that I am one of her main female role-models. Valerie's explanation truly touched my heart, "Since I've met you, Shellie, I feel that you're an inspiration to me. I've seen how you're able to balance having children, a family, other obligations, a career and helping people. I think that's so important, so I do absolutely look up to you for that."

Valerie gave Empowering Women Radio tips for getting into business, "One of the biggest, most important things I did was really network and I got myself out into the community and meet new people. Talking to people about my business is so important, because word of mouth and being able to get your name recognized is essential in a new business. A lot of 'women-owned' business owners have learned to sort of leverage different parts of who they are."

When it comes to running a business, Valerie emphasized the importance of perseverance, "I think the first thing is don't give up. It's going to take time to start anything, and you really have to have faith in yourself and move forward. Also, any new business needs to get out there. You know, you can't just sit back and expect that things are going to come to you."

Valerie has a full time job, kids and a husband, does a ton of charity work and is running her business; all the while working towards her MBA at the same time. We talked about how to balance the day-to-day. Valerie explained, "You are going to have to really prioritize and have good organizational skills. I would encourage you; if you don't feel that you have those skills, but you want to move forward with your own business or balancing all these things, ask for help and support. Even hire a consultant or mentor to help you get through it, because you really do need that support, especially if you don't have those skills. It's difficult; it's something you have to work at. That's what I would like to tell women… don't give up!"

Chapter 5:

Wellness and Joy

Sipping mulled cider and devouring delicious sweet crepes overfilled with cherries and cream, we began to reminisce. I hadn't seen Susan "Suzie" Luck in 25 years. We recalled our early teenage years. We kept sighing and realizing that we had become, dare it say it... "grown-ups". It was refreshing to have this history; to sit together and talk about the amazing and heartbreaking things that had occurred in our past. She said, "It is as if nothing has changed and at the same time"... and we both said in harmony, "everything has". Our friendship had not really skipped a beat.

We talked about this book that you are holding in your hands and the journey that brought me to it. Suzie said to me, "From my stand point, you must live big while you can." She has MS and it has been debilitating for her. She is still the vibrant and lovely Suzie I once knew and yet, she is unable to live the life she used to live. I realized while chatting with my lovely friend from my past that our wellness and joy are often interconnected.

Dr. Judy Staveley:

The Platform Magazine, Latin Connection Magazine, and a Biology Professor

It's easy for me to talk to fellow professor Dr. Judy because we both completely understand fulfilling multiple careers and life roles, "It's time management. We both have doctorates in our field, we've always had to juggle life and we had to work. We had to study. I think if you're similar to me, you can kind of understand how hard it was during those years of writing and getting published and working with your mentors, and that was time-consuming. Then it kind of eases up when you graduate, but you still stay as busy, your mind keeps going and you want to keep focusing on what you were trying to do.

"As for me, I was focused on making a change, and that was very important in my dissertation. I needed to make change for the better. My focus is on health. Time management was a big factor.

"As an athlete, training and exercising really helped me overcome some of my stressors, and it just becomes second nature after a while. The main focus is you have to love what you do."

She explained that she needs to be mindful of her commitments, "I'm the one that's investing in my career and I have a family and kids. So I do want it to succeed; however, juggling everything, as a doctor, professor and mom; I have to think about how much I can put on my plate.

"That's one thing ladies need to think about, as a mother, working, or educating… how much can you handle? People will push and push you, and I'm very motivated to succeed. I don't like personally to see things fail.

"I love to see the magazine I run getting really big, and it's very big. It's grown in the last year, and I'm very proud of that. Yet, it boils down to how much I can handle. I know where my boundaries are and that's where ladies need to understand, where are your boundaries? Don't get sick over it.

"I know some empowering women who follow us, who have discussed that they have put their heart and souls into it. They are succeeding. Yet, they have to watch so that they don't let it affect their health. If you are out of it because of sickness, you can't finish your job.

"Your health comes first. So take care of yourself. You need to exercise, take your supplements and know your boundaries of stress. Once you start feeling that's it too much, you need to step back."

During our interview, Dr. Judy and I started to talk a bit about keeping up our looks as we age. All women want to do this gracefully. "Well, I am 42, and honestly, I have not done any Botox ®, Restylane ®, Juvederm ®. I have been offered, of course, because my friends are doctors, but I have not done anything. The only thing I do is microdermabrasion, which takes the top layer of the skin off, I do a scrub that you can do at home, and then I do creams. I've done a light retinol over-the-counter.

"Other than that, to be honest, my grandmother has beautiful skin, and we're Spanish, so I hope to take after her. My grandmother is 95 years old and still living, and she barely has any wrinkles.

"However, you know, I do take care of my skin. I do read Dr. Kristin Eastman's articles in *The Platform Magazine*. We separated paths in med school, but she does teach me a lot about the basics on how to take care of your skin, and that's what we publish in the magazine monthly. I learn from her articles, the basic steps of just moisturizing, and she tells me, 'You've got to moisturize every single day, moisturize.' Every morning, I'll moisturize now just with an everyday facial cream, so that's all I really do; but I'm sure eventually I might end up Botoxing. I know a lot of my friends who do, but I think Botox is actually kind of being eliminated in the dermatology. The beauty world has newer stuff that's coming out like Juvederm and Restylane. Dr. Kristin was talking about that last month in some of our magazines."

Dr. Judy urges us, 'to look and feel our best, we need to give back as well.' She said, "Don't be greedy thinking 'I want to succeed only and not help others.' There's a lot of that out there in our society. You have to give and take. If you don't give and take, you're not going to move forward. You really need that audience and other entrepreneurs that are successful to help each other keep climbing that ladder."

Rachel Martin:

Finding Joy

I met Rachel Martin as she was keynoting the MomCon. As the keynote speaker, she was sharing her experience raising her seven children as a single mother, while blogging about "Finding Joy", and running a company called Blogging Concentrated.

Rachel recalled realizing she needed to be finding joy in even the rough times during one of her son's hospital stays, "He is diagnosed with Celiac Disease. He was really ill and we didn't know what was going on, and I remember being in the hospital at night, and he was in the hospital bed. He was a baby, and I could hear, all of a sudden, the 'blip, blip blip' of the heart monitor.

"At that moment, I realized that there were Mamas and Dads in that hospital that would have given anything to hear a heartbeat, so I needed to be thankful for it. It was a horrible time, but I needed to be thankful.

"I just started listing every single thing I was thankful for, from the IV in his arm to the nurses bringing me gluten-free stuff. That's what finding joy is, knowing that there's something that we can be thankful for even in the difficult times."

Rachel and I had a very interesting conversation about the modern day concerns that arise when we compare our everyday lives with what others choose to show on social media. Rachel Martin explained, "When we compare, our own life all of sudden, doesn't seem to measure up to the expectation.

"We live in a world where there's Facebook and social media, and it's like a highlight reel of everybody's lives. If we compare our everyday lives to that, then no doubt our own happiness and joy is whittled away. Focus less on comparing and more about embracing each of us where we truly are on our own journeys.

"I once wrote an article that was in Huffington Post that was, The Mom Confession. I wrote really simple things like, 'I don't always feed my kids organic apples,' or 'We serve boxed macaroni and cheese for dinner or I have a sock basket where everyone just digs for their socks,' and it was just really this, like real life stuff that all of us moms face.

"I feel like, everybody knows that when you get the call that in five minutes someone is coming over, that the goal is to quickly get a basket, shove everything into the basket and put it in the room in the basement. We all have a hidden room, but we don't talk about it. Yeah, don't go in that room. That's the storage room, but we all know it's like, 'that's where all the junk is', so the mom confession was about that.

"What struck me about it the most was, I had a couple of people that said, 'How can you endorse boxed macaroni and cheese?' I realized at that moment the judging that we have in our culture. I wrote a rebuttal post that says, 'why boxed macaroni and cheese does not define motherhood.' I reminded my readers that there are some moms out there that would do anything for a box of macaroni and cheese in their cupboard, because that would be the only food they have for their kids. The second we decide that we put a label or a ruler on motherhood, and decide that you're a really good mom if you only serve this type of macaroni and cheese, we are missing who the women are at their cores."

I was glad that Rachel Martin shared this with my listeners and I. First of all, my little man adores Kraft Macaroni and Cheese ®. More importantly, as a mother myself, I feel that this is such a ridiculous debate, especially when I just finished a conversation with a single mother living in Africa who has had to literally beg on the streets to provide food for her child to eat. She and I both agreed that when you are in a survival position, we would do anything for our children. She is active on social media with me and I can only imagine what she would think reading a shaming article about serving a child any form of nourishment.

The "Mommy Bloggers" who I interviewed for *Common Threads,* spend a great deal of time online and are very in tune with the issue of "mom shaming" in online communities. Obviously, in the ideal virtual world and in person, women would build each other up through support.

"I think that so often, we as women add the word 'just' in front of what we do. We say, 'I'm just a mom. I just did this.' We dismiss everything that we do, and to live empowered means that wherever state you are in life; if you're a mom, at that moment, you are a mom, and that is a huge thing. You don't need to minimize that you are a mom by putting the word 'just' in front of it.

"You don't need to minimize. We minimize what we do. A friend says, 'Oh, your hair looks nice.' We just minimize it replying with, 'Oh, I just slept in it just right.' We are so easy to dismiss the awesome that we have inside.

"On the flip side, I look at my five-year-old, and he loves being awesome! I say, 'Look at that,' and he'll sing the 'Everything is Awesome' song from the Lego Movie." Kids get it and don't minimize.

Rachel explained The Dear Mom Letters, "They are letters that started out on my site. They began as these really simple letters, and went crazy viral. The moms just ended up loving them, because I think so often in our culture, we're told what we should be doing, and this is what you should you do, and there's this measuring stick that moms have.

"The first letter that I wrote that went viral was, 'Dear Mom who feels like she's failing.' Then the next line is,

'You're not. If you and I were sitting in Starbucks having a Caramel Macchiato and I was sitting across from you, I would tell you that you are not failing.'

"I went on and listed the reasons why. Society tells us as moms we should do this Pinterest project, and you should do this, and you should do that, but at the end of the day when I'm 80, I'm not going to remember any of that stuff! What I'm going to remember are the moments that I sit up at 3:00 a.m. rocking a baby or studying with my child when they didn't get math facts and I just sat there over and over and over again. I said, those are the things that are going to matter. It's not all this expectations; it's about those simple, simple moments, and I really ended it with a cry saying to moms, 'You can do this. You can do this.' Replace 'I'm failing' with, 'I can do this.'"

I spoke to Rachel the night before she keynoted at the MomCon to talk to the audience about finding their joy. She mentioned, "So often we're told, 'You can't do this. You won't measure up,' and I'm going to start out tomorrow talking about excuses. If we live by the excuses, we don't get to feel like we are enough and whole. I just don't want women and moms to live by the excuses or to live thinking that they're not enough, because they're measuring themselves by what society says versus what is really important.

"I love talking to people one-on-one and inspiring people to just take a chance, articulating the dream. Don't lose yourself. Go for those things in life. Do not judge yourself based on everything that you think you should be doing, but really start to see all the awesome that you already have inside. I think it's a lot of shedding of the layers that we've been told of who we are as women and starting to love the gifts that we each can bring to the table.

"To live empowered means that we appreciate what we do in our lives every single day. Know that it makes a difference and not adding the word 'just', and, honestly, not letting fear have any type of filter in what we do. I have lived with fear and I know how it can cripple. It is important to learning how to push it to the side.

"I once wrote a post called 'Why We Need to Stop Saying: How Do You Do It All?'. Because when someone asks that question, it's oftentimes not even a reflection. First of all, the person receiving it can say, 'Well, how do I do it all? What in the world are you talking about?' You get this sense of doubt like 'what in the world am I doing?'

"But also the person who is asking is probably insecure herself. Instead, I would encourage women to say, 'I love what you're doing with your kids. It's awesome how you do it. I love what you do with the birthday parties,' and just stop doing the comparison thing.

"I really believe that to live empowered is really about knowing you are doing what you can do in this world. Sometimes for some people, it means getting up in the middle of the night with a newborn, and there is never a 'just' with that. That is an awesome thing to do, and it makes a life difference."

Rachel Martin's purpose has been realized, "I really have a deep, deep passion for helping women. Passion for showing women how to not live in fear of expectations of what other people tell them they should be. I have this strong sense of that.

"Truthfully, I believe that we are all here on this earth with a deep purpose. We need to start believing in ourselves and doing one thing at a time. Just one thing well and move forward, knowing that what we did is enough.

"Then beyond that, we need to be able to be free to articulate our dreams, to look at a friend and say, 'You know what? I believe in you.' I want to leave people with the freedom to articulate their dreams and also the deep, deep, passion and desire to live a joyful life, knowing that you can embrace this moment for what it is. You don't have to love every single second of it, (like if the kids are puking), but there's something about it that is deep down a gift."

Rachel discussed the importance of connecting with other ladies, "I would like to say that I, myself, have received mentoring. Many women in my life have basically taken me under their wing and showed me the way to go, educational-wise, as well as, relationship-wise.

"And one of my biggest mentors (my mom is going to be shocked that I said it) is my mother. She's one of my spiritual leaders, and I'll go into other leaders that I have as well, but she has been my greatest role model, my greatest mentor spiritually, because she's an ordained minister. She steps outside of that mother mode at times, and she just tells me, spiritually, the guidance that you would get from a pastor, from a minister.

"I really appreciated the times where she would every morning, (even today), call me before I would head in to work and she would talk to me and we would pray. We would say the Lord's Prayer every single morning to this day. That started in school, and so just having that support and that spiritual guidance to know that before you start your busy day, you acknowledge who gave you life. That's been the most encouraging thing that's lead me to engage in, mentoring others, being able to have that guidance and that extra push and that extra oomph every day."

Rachel described how spending time in Haiti profoundly influenced her; "2013 in Haiti changed my life. It rocked my world. When I was in Haiti, there was no spirit of comparison among women. There was instead this awesome hand-in-hand, arm-in-arm linking.

"I give my sons this example, that if I wanted to push you over and have one stand there, and if I was going to push you over, look how quickly and easily I could do it. Then I'll say, 'link your arm with your brother', and I'll tell his brother, 'don't let Caleb fall over', and they work together and it gets harder, but by the time all my kids are all linked together, the one that I said I didn't want to move, they don't move. This is because everybody is working together at that moment, and that was the culture when I was in Haiti.

"The women did not care what someone else was wearing or what their house was like. Rather it was more about embracing each other in their journey. They really come alongside and see each other for who they really are. It is not about all the externals."

I asked Rachel Martin, "How do we do that in our American culture?" She replied, "In findingjoy.net and on my Facebook page; they know that I'm not about comparisons. They know that there is no 'I'm a stay-at-home' versus 'working at home' mom. There's no 'single mom' versus 'married mom'. There is no judging because I think the second we start to judge, we start to create this unrealistic expectation. We create anxiety and angst.

"I tell moms all the time; your friend comes over and your house is a mess and you say, 'Oh, I'm so sorry, it's messy, like, you know, kind of messy.' You are setting the stage so that when they come to your house to visit you, it has to be clean, versus just saying, 'Come in, this is our life. We're welcoming you.'

"When I was in Haiti, the women never said, 'I'm so sorry for my dirt floor.' They just said, 'Please come in and sit down. We're so glad you're here.' So I think if we can do that as women and just say, 'I'm so glad you're here,' and not have to put the precedent and expectation so high… we're freer as women to love each other."

Chapter 6:

Connections

Traveling back from one of my speaking adventures, Margaret "Maggie" Schoenholtz shuffled into the middle seat on the plane next to me. As she prepared her tea anticipating the seven-hour flight, she accidentally spilled it. As we scrambled to clean it up, we began to chat in-between her adorable apologies.

We quickly bonded and I learned about her life as a university student, her sister's Make-A-Wish Foundation trip before she had a liver transplant, and her pageant win as Miss Asian Global/Miss Asian America.

She was thrilled to learn about the Common Threads trilogy and the work I have been doing with the Global Sisterhood. After our discussion and we returned to our homes, she connected me with her mentor Francis Kong who is an inspiring author and speaker.

You never know where chance meetings will take you! Because I met Maggie, I will be presenting as a keynote speaker at the Imagine Talks at University of California, Berkeley University (led by Francis Kong) to inspire students to find and meet their life goals.

Connections can have life-long impact on yourself and others... when especially when you pay them forward.

Demeatria Boccella:

Fashion Africana

The thunderous drumbeats echoing through the August Wilson Center prepared the audience for the ethic explosion on the runway. The African fabrics, stunning diverse models, and the colors brought the splendor of Africa to set the scene.

The evening of Fashion Africana was packed with art, fashion and photography that wowed the audience with images from Africa. I had the opportunity to interview Paris-based photographer, Mario Epanya, who had a collection of amazing photography titled Glamazonia. This exhibit celebrates black beauty through hairstyles and ceremonial dress.

We talked at Demeatria's Fashion Africana event on camera about Mario's "Vogue Africa" exhibit. Believe it or not, there is a Vogue magazine that represents every continent except the continent of Africa. Mario presented what could be if we embraced black beauty by creating fictitious Vogue Africa covers and posting them online. They went viral, and then he also included these images as part of a proposal to obtain a license to publish a Vogue Africa.

The proposal was denied; however, the editor of Vogue Italia interviewed Mario. Demeatria explained to Empowering Women Radio, "I read that interview, and that's how we connected via social media. His images were just so powerful, and they made a huge statement, and folks thought, 'Oh, my God, there's a Vogue Africa now;' there was a lot of excitement and enthusiasm. We want to see more black beauty, gracing the covers of our favorite fashion magazines."

I recall another time when I saw Demeatria. This time she was presenting at Macy's downtown as the keynote speaker. Who could miss her stunning features and her fabulous hair-less head? Demeatria was in the front of the event that I modeled in to raise funds for E-Magnify (which is an organization for women entrepreneurs). I remember posing behind her on the stage, wearing the Ralph Lauren summer collection as she talked.

Demeatria explained to the ladies about starting out reading the fashion magazines and dreaming of modeling for them someday. Unfortunately, she did not see dark skin being represented at the time. She could imagine a day when she would be able to see multiple women of color on the covers of the top magazines.

When she was older, she began to reach out to individuals who were working in the industry and looked to them as mentors, to learn about the work that they did in the field. Demeatria volunteered several times for Mercedes-Benz's fashion week in NY and met many people within the industry.

She encourages us to seek out mentors. Reflecting on a connection with one of her fashion heroes, Demeatria said, "I recall reading one story on Norma Kamali in Oprah's *O Magazine* when it was first published and arranged as a luncheon with her. It was interesting, because I was always very ambitious and I wasn't afraid to ask for support or guidance. I met a lot of individuals who were just willing to reach out and help, which led to more exposure. I became sure that I wanted to get into the production side of fashion.

"One of my mentors, Monique Greenwood, the former editor-in-chief of *Essence Magazine*, gave me the opportunity to witness a whole Essence cover photo shoot and she connected me with her colleagues. It was just so great to be able to learn that side of the industry, as well as the publishing side, and get an inside view of just how things are produced and put together."

Demeatria has had multiple mentors over the years but feels she would be remiss if she didn't give credit to the very first individual who really nurtured her desire and interest in fashion. Demeatria discussed her mentor, "Yvette was a Pittsburgh-based model, who was an amazing African-American woman. She was just a regal individual, and I always admired her, her beauty and her presence; she took me under her wing and really nurtured that interest, exposed me to the industry, and I learned so much through her."

If you are wondering how to obtain a mentor, Demeatria says, "All you have to do is just ask. Nine times out of ten, people will help you because they want to give back and pay it forward."

Now she has the opportunity to share what she has learned and share her passion with young people through FashionAFRICANA's educational programming. Two years ago, in conjunction with the Glamazonia exhibition, they launched an educational program that they take into the schools and various community after-school programs; they engage young people through fashion. Also, they have the opportunity to implement a portion of that program in New York to young girls from twenty-eight New York City high schools and colleges.

One of the fashionable examples of connections and collaborations between the Global Sisterhood of Empowering Women happened very naturally and involved Demeatria. As you may recall, Aissata Camara and her sister, Mariama Camara's story of bringing the tie-dye fabrics, from Guinea, Africa to the runways of NY Fashion Week to support funding their non-profit, 'There Is No Limit.'

When the Camara sisters came into Pittsburgh to be on my show, 'Inspiring Lives with Dr. Shellie', they met Alice Beckett-Rumberger, who is the mother of seven who runs businesses, such as Therafusion and sits on multiple boards. Alice is now an ambassador for 'There Is No Limit Foundation'. Alice is such a natural networker that she procured Mariama's fabrics for Demeatria's latest Fashion Africana.

I was grinning as I sat in the front row for the fashion show in the spectacular Carnegie Museum of Natural History, as the runway was transformed by the beauty of the tie-dyes and the glamour of Africa. Demeatria's childhood dreams of African women having their beauty represented in fashion, is happening due in part to her talent as a producer and her incredible international connections.

Kelly Hadous:
Win the Room

I met Kelly Hadous at a women's empowerment summit in New York. I sensed that she had a flair for communicating the instant we began to chat. Because of our love for speaking and empowering women, we hit it off right away. I have taught doctoral classes at the Ph.D. level at Robert Morris University for a decade in the Global Perspective, so I was intrigued by her work with communicating through cultural boundaries.

Kelly Hadous, is the CEO and founder of Win The Room™. She is a certified executive coach, international public speaker and communication strategist at heart. She has a background in finance, speech and drama, including work as a 'classically-trained' actor in stage and film. Kelly was on Wall Street's front line at the young age of 19 and became a Series 7 & 63 securities trader. After that, she earned degrees from Columbia University and studied Shakespeare and Chekhov at The Royal Academy of Dramatic Arts in London.

Some of her many recent speaking engagements include TEDx, Women's Leadership Conference, Women in Tech, Trailblazing Women, National Cultural Women's Conference, New York University Global Conference, and the Rock The World Conference. She is a very well-spoken lady.

Kelly explained Win the Room, "It started out as public speaking, but then it went into many different directions, within communications. It encompasses leadership, team development, just being a better leader. It helps clients articulate thoughts more clearly and effectively. Also, it encompasses social media marketing.

"I teach c-level executives, managers, entrepreneurs and leaders internationally, to be successful. It takes coaching. It takes skill, practice and it takes delivery. It is important that we find our authentic voice—your real story and appeal. Then it must be communicated credibly, creatively and confidently.

"I've done many interviews for our Win the Room media venture. My favorites have been centered around when people can really open up, and I can see the inner-workings of their mind. We figure out why they are so good at what they do, either why are they a great communicator or why they are fabulous at sales or something like that.

"I think it all boils down to how one motivates another person or a large group to do what they want them to do, while creating a win/win situation.

"I interviewed a woman from India, who was a change agent. She was very high up with the education system. At the time, there weren't many women in her position or even in the leadership of that institution. She really rose up despite the many challenges.

"I find it fascinating when someone opens up and you discover the hardships and the challenges that they overcame and that they got where they wanted to be in life.

"There is a difference in communication when you speak with different people from different cultures, but I think at some point, the world will start to melt together a little bit more. Communication is crossing borders extremely quickly, but I do see a difference. For example, right now, I'm developing a new company, and I have to talk to people who are creating the technology. I've talked to developers in this country and in other countries; I have found that it's very different how the communication is perceived in different parts of the world.

"In some of the situations that I've run into, when I'm trying to talk to developers in other countries (let's say India), the conversation there needs to be very straightforward, to the point and without a whole lot of emotion in it. They just need to get from point A to point B. They want to know, 'What do I need to do?' and it has to be precise.

"Whereas, when I talk to developers in this country, there can be more emotion in it. You know, that's probably the cultural barrier. Even though I'm in communications, I'm not fully aware of their cultural environment, so I have to be careful in the way that I relate my objective to them.

"I have a little bit more leniency in this country, because I get the people more: we come from kind of the same dynamic. We understand our way of being. I'm not entirely sure sometimes when I'm talking to people in other countries, their typical ways.

"That is just one part of it, but you see it all over the world. You see it in China. You see it everywhere; how people respond to people differently and how people respond to authority figures differently. There are multiple approaches.

"When you are speaking, make sure that you reach three goals. First, know your objective for 'the talk' and what you truly want to impart to your audience; once you know the end goal, back up and determine the steps to get them there. Have a clear strategy in place.

"Second, know your audience and determine why they are there, and finally, bring yourself to the place, the table, to the room; so you can in fact Win the Room. Finally, make them feel good, show them some love and draw them into your story and strategies for success. You can and you will, Win the Room!"

Beth Caldwell:
Leadership Academy for Women

Beth Caldwell is an inspirational speaker who helps women discover their purpose and share their talents with the world. She is a popular author and writes for the *Pittsburgh Business Times* newspaper and *Smart Business Magazine.* She is a Global Instructor for the Steve Harvey Success Institute where she teaches business and life strategies to students from around the globe. Beth is best known as the founder of Pittsburgh Professional Women and Leadership Academy for Women. Her books include *I Wish I'd Known THAT! Secrets to Success in Business, Inspired Entrepreneurs, EMPOWER, INSPIRE,* and the newly released book *Smart Leadership.*

Beth shared more about her company, "I started my business out of necessity, I was divorced with 2 young sons, and my youngest was experiencing serious medical issues. I absolutely needed to have a flexible schedule and, frankly, I needed profits - not wages. I was a single mom of a child with a disability. No one plans on a divorce. I had to reinvent my life from welfare to well-off.

"The Leadership Academy for Women is the most important thing I've ever done. It's so rewarding to watch this small group of women blossom in each session. We begin with 15 women who are already significantly accomplished, I get to see them stretch and achieve more than they imagined was possible. The most important thing is that they are able to influence the women they work with in their offices and communities, which creates a perpetual movement.

"Leadership Academy for Women is a place where women gain the courage to step into their purpose. It's where they gain confidence and learn strategies to help them to overcome conflict, navigate change, negotiate important issues, develop other leaders and create a legacy. This 12-week program is not taught from a textbook. It is taught by women who offer practical strategies after they have navigated real-life issues.

"In my first Leadership Academy, a young woman, a graduate of CMU registered. I'd never met her and didn't know her at all. She called and asked me if I could offer a payment plan for her tuition and I did. She had never had the opportunity to be in a room with a diverse group of women leaders. She gained so much confidence during the first few weeks of our academy that she applied for and interviewed for her dream job in Manhattan.

"We had a quick mentoring session before her final interview and she was able to negotiate additional benefits and a moving allowance. She and I keep in touch as she navigates her career and she mentors other women in turn.

She is just one of the women who've made big changes and taken big steps in forwarding her life and career.

"My biggest networking tip is the opposite from what you typically hear. I actually recommend to many women that they stop networking. Sometimes we're so busy networking that we don't have time to nurture our existing relationships. Men don't do that! Set aside specific time each month to nurture your network. Arrange to meet with people on certain days of the month, or host a regular session in your office.

"In my personal life, I'm really rewarded when my sons emulate my values. There's nothing more rewarding than to see my sons making a difference in the world. They have both turned out to be strong leaders and men of great influence.

"Ladies, don't beat yourself up for what you're not doing. That has been my biggest mistake. Acknowledge yourself for what you have accomplished and remember that you can do it all, you just can't do it all at the same time."

Erin Bagwell:
Dream, Girl Documentary

Erin Bagwell, is producing the movie 'Dream, Girl' which is a documentary showcasing the stories of ambitious and inspiring female entrepreneurs. Clinique ™ and the makers of the TED Talks profiled Erin as an inspiring entrepreneur. During the clip, Erin tells the story of walking into her corporate job very proud of her hard work, and the only feedback she received from her supervisor was that she looked pretty that day. This was a turning point inside of her. She realized that she needed to live her dreams, to find out what successful women entrepreneurs in New York were doing, and share that with the world through Dream, Girl.

Erin described the Kickstarter campaigns: for both, the Dream, Girl Documentary and the one that funded the Common Threads book series that you are now reading. Erin Bagwell stated, "I think the great thing about crowd funding is that anyone can put out a project or idea and with a lot of hard work and energy, they can see the impact of their mission. The amazing thing about our Kickstarter campaigns is that women not only believed in our projects, but also were willing to put their money on it. Women are an economic force. So seeing that power on a woman centric project is inspiring.

"Crowd funding is something that's so tricky and it was such a learning experience for me and I feel so grateful that we were able to double our goal. That was definitely something that I was always hoping for; yet, I am still totally in shock that it has happened. I mean, essentially, it's figuring out who your audience is and trying to get to them what they need in a really big way.

"I had a lot of help. I did a lot of press. I took a lot of meetings to get it out there to as many different avenues as possible, and I will say that the fabulous Marie Forleo's network really pushed us over the edge! Once she shared it within her newsletter and shared it with her followers, that was really the tipping point for us and really sent us to go viral. I have nothing but the utmost gratitude and love for her, because she really kind of took the project under her wing and shared it.

"I've been really lucky that, in the Kickstarter community, there are a bunch of women who have produced films. I have definitely got on the phone with every female documentary artist that I could! The narrow image of women we see in the media now just doesn't satisfy the dimension and complexity of real women. It's vital to showcase more of these stories because it's transformative to the audience and the creators, to have women sharing their stories.

"Sarah Moshman from the Empowerment Project has been hugely helpful in helping us; when I had questions about Executive Producer titles or roles, or how to set up my company, should I be a C Corp, all those kinds of details that, as a creative person, sometimes, can go over my head. She was super helpful because she had been through the process a year before when she created a documentary.

"I feel very lucky that women have definitely been supportive in helping me through the process, and there have been a lot of male mentors as well. My friend Mark runs a company called Flood. Every time over the last five years, I have had questions about investors and things like that, I have worked with Mark; so I consider him to be a huge asset and a huge help as well.

"I've always considered myself entrepreneurial. I've really struggled with seeing myself as a leader, as we don't see those images of women (being CEO's and running businesses in the media), so I was really drawn to creating something that would inspire other women to see that in themselves.

"I live in New York City and there are amazing networking opportunities for women here and globally. Once I started meeting all those female founders, I didn't feel like a blogger anymore, I felt like a founder.

"I felt, that if these women I am spending time with are empowering me to see myself in a different light, then imagine if a dozen entrepreneurs put all of their wisdom and their advice together. So, I saw the power of that, and I just felt like I was really called to create it.

"I love film. I'm so in love with seeing the image of things as it runs across the screen or in a theater. There's something so romantic about a film, and I think it's truly the most powerful media we have. I mean it's one thing to read something or to have somebody tell you advice, but to actually see them living their mission; their life is incredible. For example, to be able to feel Mariama Camara's energy, seeing her and the way she talks to me; it's so much more impactful. I felt really, really inspired to do it. I studied film in college and I produced a slew of short films and a 32-minute documentary, so I felt very connected to the medium as well.

"One of the incredible women that we interviewed for Dream, Girl was Clara Villarosa, the President of Villarosa Media. Clara is an 83-year-old entrepreneur on her third business. Her story really struck me because she didn't start her first company until she was 53 years old. She hit the glass ceiling at her job. Then, Clara got a buyout, which gave her a little bit of money to start a bookstore, HueMan books. Once she started the bookstore, she really found her voice, and it became her passion.

"My advice is to really just get started, get the ball rolling, and see how people react to it. You know, we took the first steps to start the trailer for the Kickstarter, so that was like a three minute snippet, I interviewed three different companies for it and we were able to figure out that you know, the audio didn't work this time.

"What are the things that work and what are the things that don't work? We had to figure this out first. So, before diving into this huge documentary that costs thousands and thousands of dollars, I was able to kind of create a micro set and figure out what worked and what didn't. Working with an all-female crew did work. It was really helpful for me to kind of take the first step and do like whatever the smallest piece is, and then we have to build from there."

Erin went on to discuss her conception of feminism, "Feminism can mean so many things to different people. For me, it's about gender equality, the political, social and economic equality of the sexes. It is figuring out what works for you. There are a lot of mixed messages from the media and within our culture, about the role that women should play.

"I think that having a feminist mindset allows me especially to be able to decipher what truly works for me, as opposed to just going with the flow and what would be considered the norm. I love being a feminist, and I think it's something that everyone should explore. Once I tapped in to feminism and figured out my role and how it works for me, it has just empowered me in such amazing ways and I feel really thankful that I found feminism actually.

"I am embarrassed to say I wasn't a feminist growing up and I really regret not taking gender studies classes in college. I had very traditional preconceived ideas about what the word meant. I thought maybe men weren't invited to the conversation, or it was kind of about women only which it's not; it's really focused on gender-roles.

"When I moved to New York City about 5 years ago, I kind of became bombarded with all of the huge advertisements you see of women and what women should look like, and this kind of weird perfected ideal; it really affected me, being surrounded by those images.

"You walk outside and there's catcalling. New York is kind of a weird place for women. I was kind of was recognizing those objectified images and I started reading about it online.

"I started reading Jezebel and other feminist blogs and kind of getting connected with the feminist community, and then kind of learning how to combat it. I started recognizing that the images are photo-shopped. They are not realistic images of women. My worth isn't in how long my legs are or how airbrushed my skin is. It was empowering to take a step back from what I see daily and being able to filter those kind of everyday things that happen, just by being a commuter.

"Don't get me wrong; I'm a visual person. I love great lighting and I think like a little bit of retouching is fine, we want people to look their best, but when you are distorting an image. Or cropping people's size and arms, then we have a bigger problem on our hands."

Erin explained how to get a dream out of your head and make it happen, "When you are trying to bring fruition to a big project, start small. Build on the tiny momentums and the positive energy that comes with the idea. Don't expect to see immediate results overnight. Every seed takes time to grow. Use that time to polish, perfect and master your craft. It's really hard work to get something off the ground; but if it's your passion, it will inspire you. Keep going!

"My dream for the girls of the world is that we have a more diverse representation in the media so women can see themselves as whatever is their heart's desire to be. There is so much more inside of us, I want to see these women leaders on screens around the world inspiring and uplifting."

Chapter 7:

Style

The classiness of a triple strand of pearls, a brilliant pop of color on a scarf, loosely draped around a neck or the elegance of the red sole of a Louboutin heel. These are all external style points that speak volumes when a woman walks into a room.

I have had the opportunity to strut on the runways of many fashion shows over the years to raise funds for everything from the Go Red campaign to the Pittsburgh Zoo. I know the transforming power of fashion and finding individual style. When I was inducted into the Fashion Hall of Fame as the Exceptional Artist, I stood in front of the Omni William Penn and discussed the many ways that fashion had affected my spirit and persona.

Yet, sometimes the power of style simply comes down to the days when I felt like I was a hot mess and grabbed that 'go to little black dress'. I then felt I could take on the world again. The ladies in this chapter (and many throughout this series) are involved in the fashion industry and have a powerful way of helping others feel and look their best.

Beth Shari:
Hollywood Glam

A combo of pinup and pixie; she's my Mary Poppins, who can pull almost anything out of her magical bag at a moment's notice. Beth Shari has been backstage with me for years. From managing wardrobe on the TV set for Inspiring Lives with Dr. Shellie to creating elaborate costumes for my characters on stage; Beth is someone I can count on to have everything from a shoulder to cry on to a bobby pin.

Watching her in action at the International Missing Piece Calendar shoot was fabulous. Her niche area in fashion is bringing to life, Hollywood Glam fashions and lingerie from the 1920s to the 40s. She has a gentle way about her that encourages ladies to love the body they are in, and shows them how they can feel their most beautiful.

During the Fabulous Forties fundraiser for the Homeless Children's Education Fund, Hollywood Glam lit up the runway bringing dazzling retro-inspired designs.

Her custom-made creations enhance each client's natural beauty. The models on stage radiated confidence and sass.

Not all women feel confident in the body they are born with or develop into. Particularly, those who have gone through life-events like childbirth or menopause can feel this way. Furthermore, today's connected world of constant media consumption can make it very easy for women to compare themselves to others and can lead to decreased self-esteem.

Beth is a strong believer in loving the body you have and believes that personal style can be an amazing confidence-booster. Beth asserts that, "All body types are beautiful, not just the ones that social media and magazines inundate with as the ideal. Finding the fashion that compliments your body type will make a difference in how you walk, talk and think.

"There was a time, not too long ago, when women didn't leave their home without wearing a hat and gloves. Now it is socially acceptable to be seen in pajama bottoms and tank tops. Restaurants and theaters that once used to be a special occasion to dress up, now accept customers in jeans and 'casual' attire. What you wear shows the world how you feel about yourself, whether it is conscious or subconscious. So if you feel its ok to habitually not shower and wear bedroom slippers in public, you should re-think your daily routine. I understand that people have busy lives but still try to find ways to put yourself first."

Beth Shari explains how to find our own inner pin-up, "There truly is something magical about putting on a sexy bra or silky stockings. You always want to start at your foundation and build your image outward from there." She reminds us that it is like playing a role on stage. The actor can learn the lines and know where to go physically but until they slip on the costume, they don't fully become the character. When you open the velvet curtain on your day to step into life's stage, make sure that you are projecting the most fabulous version of yourself.

Jackie Capatolla:
Jacqueline's Salon

Backstage at fashion shows there is always a buzz in the air. The models are chatting about everything and taking selfies on their phones. The designers are doing last minute prep work, getting the ladies styled and sometimes even making last minute changes. It's the hair and makeup area that I love to sit and be pampered.

Few do it better than Jackie Capatolla. I know that when I sit in her chair, I will be transformed to a fabulous version of myself so that I can hit the runway to tell the story for the designer. She is an amazing hair and make-up artist with a passion for helping all ladies discover their best looks for everything, from the runway and even just for an evening out.

Jackie has prepped me for magazine, red carpet, hosting a fashion show at Macy's and much more, including fundraisers for the American Heart Association and the Make-a-Wish Foundation. The work that she does for the

Make-a-Wish Foundation is important to her because, "I wanted to be able to use my talent and my salon, and for the people in my industry to all come together and have a makeover for a young child that may be going through some hardships. It has been a great experience for all of those who were involved."

She has been in business, owning Jacqueline's Salon for 20 years, a milestone that carries with it according to Jacqueline, "A lot of ups and downs; but I just continue to move forward. I've always felt that in any business you're going to be times when you have challenges. If you keep pushing through them and keep working toward what it is that you really want… your passion, your dream, all of that… you're going to get through those hard times and the good times are going to overtake the hard times."

Jackie Capatolla has also written a book called *Shear Dreams*, which was based on, "… a vision that I had. I started to take notes of all the experiences I had in the salon after 20 years in business. Even going back to before I owned the salon, I had drawings of what I thought my salon would look like some day. I kept all of my writing since I was 16-years-old. One day, it just clicked in my head that I have all of this information in my journals; why not turn it into a book? This way I could share it with other people to help them to learn from my knowledge and my experience.

My readers don't necessarily have to be in the beauty industry. I feel that this book is an inspiration, and would help motivate anybody to follow their dreams; no matter what their goal is. It's a book that's going to encourage you to keep going, to follow your dreams and to find your passion."

Like the best hairdressers and bartenders, she is an amazing person to spill your guts to. She gets it and builds ladies up in her chair by making them feel beautiful outside to match the inside. Jackie explains, "Of course, we're not licensed therapists, but, I have seen everything from divorce, death, and cancer. I've had many people cry in my chair. The reasons range from losing their pets to shaving people's heads because they have cancer.

I've cried with them. We really do become, not so much a therapist to them, but a support system to them. It's nice if we have a couple words of advice or words to make them feel better about themselves."

What does Jackie love the most about the beauty industry? "I can make other people feel good about themselves. I love seeing my client's facial expressions when they have a new look or a new style. When you are behind that chair, that person becomes not just a client; they become your friend. They are reliant on you for any issues that they have in their lives. They just open up and they feel relaxed. We have a special gift that we give to people to help them feel better, inside and out. That's my motto. 'Jacqueline's inside and out' to make them feel better."

We women are always multi-tasking; so during my interview on Empowering Women Radio, when the timer went off on my hair dye, as I was trying to get my grays covered while chatting on the radio… We started laughing. Jacqueline said through the giggles, when it was obvious to the listeners that we weren't in a quiet studio: "Anytime I deal with Shellie, it is just an experience and I love it. She is just such a joy. So I am here, yes, getting interviewed as she is getting her hair colored. I love it. It's fun.

"When you have something that you are passionate about, and you feel good about yourself, you want to make it shine through. Just like what you're doing with your books, with *Common Threads*. It's just a wonderful way to embrace all of the women out there that experience and share their dreams and their passions... and you're bringing this together, which is just absolutely amazing. We all love you for that. We all need each other. Women need each other to build each other up. You don't need competition with each other. You need to help each other to bring each other to a better place.

"Women are powerful people. We all have to come together and stick together. Yes, you have challenges; you have issues that come up, but you know what? Push through them. Work through them. Keep moving. Always be strong.

"I do believe that we have to have a support system that is around us. I have a wonderful family that I love and that is always there for me, and so are my friends. Not everyone has a big family, not everyone has a lot of friends, but be sure you have somebody in your life that you can count on and go to for support. Don't ever be afraid to ask for that help. If you're having trouble, if you're having issues, just keep asking for that help, keep moving forward and believe in yourself."

Debi Weiss:
International Fashion Forum

When I stepped onto the runway wearing an amazing natural fiber lace gown at Pittsburgh Fashion Week, I felt the eyes on the design. I knew that Debi Weiss' collection was a hit. Being the lead model the same year I was inducted into the Fashion Hall of Fame; it was a surreal experience. The camera light bulbs were flashing like crazy!

Excitedly, the audience whispered about the pure spectacle as the gymnast did flips and the dancers pirouetted down the over 100-foot runway at the Highmark Stadium. What was on the media's mind though, was the International Fashion Forum spearheaded by Debi Weiss' fashion choices for the runway.

Debi Weiss has seen the world through her decades as a flight attendant. "I've been a flight attendant for 30 years, international; yet, I've always had a business on the side. When I started working international fights, it opened doors to many other things. The beaded gowns, the alpaca fiber, and I found them while I was abroad. The fibers at the time weren't as big here in the United States. So, now the business is growing and so is the love for these fabrics here, it's a great thing." She is now the owner of the International Fashion Forum, which has a focus on natural fabrics such as alpaca from Peru.

Debi explained about the popularity of her alpaca collection. She doesn't even have to keep her store open more than two days a week because people flock to her to purchase these garments. "Alpaca is shaved from an animal and it is widely used in South America where they originated in the Indian Mountains. It is very well known in Europe, but in the United States, we didn't know a whole lot about the alpaca until ten years ago. So, it's still growing. Alpaca is the most incredible fiber you will ever have on your body."

These fabrics are created by-women for-women in remote locations. Like the old-fashioned quilting or spinning bees, the women create handicrafts in Peru while chatting and bonding. Debi explained, "I am involved in the whole process from the yarn for the fabric to the design of a product. The women sit together knitting and spinning the yarn creating sweaters, scarves, hats, dresses, and even wedding gowns... They start right from the fiber, the fiber off the animal before it's been cleaned. They feel it with their fingers to grade it...then it goes on to be cleaned and the spinning wheel, and then onto the garment."

Women in remote places are creating handicrafts such as these and being brought to America to be sold. Multiple women-owned non-profit companies then utilize some of the funds brought in from the sale of these wares to help the creators and artisans.

Many times, I have chatted privately with Debi. Since she has been in business herself for so long, she gives great advice; especially when it comes to the reality of being a woman entrepreneur. Debi gave me wonderful advice that applies to relationships and also running a business, "If in your heart you're feeling something is wrong, go with what you're feeling. I think it's a danger sign if you're getting red flags. I've gotten them before. Sometimes I've taken those red flags and say, 'Well, I got to do it anyways', and that's when I've gotten into a situation that I've had to overcome.

"So, go with what your heart is telling you, or do your research and your homework. If you're not feeling good about something, we've got so much information on the Internet. Get online and look it up. If you see something is wrong, don't do it. Change your ways. There's always Plan A, Plan B, Plan C. Also, when you go through the hard times, sometimes you just want to throw your hands up and say 'oh goodness, this is just too much,' but, you get through them. After you get through them, you know that you've grown and you made it even better than it was beforehand.

"So, those hard times turn into great experiences and make you much more wise. That's why you don't give up, because it just takes you there."

She also warns not to stretch oneself too thin. We know so many ladies who struggle with delegation. Team building needs to be a part of every business woman's plan according to Debi. She explained, "In today's world, you do see a lot of women in businesses; but, sometimes it can be tough. I think it's the greatest thing to be. It inspires me to see more and more women pop up and do things.

"Dividing time is extremely hard. Teamwork is a big help with that. Sometimes if you're married, or not married, if you've got a husband or a friend that can help you out a little bit, it is a big help. Let them help!

"We always want to do everything ourselves. You can't do everything yourself. You need to designate things to other people. You know where your needs are and where the other person's strengths are, so designate. Success is letting other people help you and putting together a good team.

"I've worked so hard for many years. I've done a lot of it. When you're small, you can do a lot of things on your own, but when you get to a certain point and you need to start letting other people help. You have to do this.

"It goes back to being a flight attendant. There are a lot of things that happen on planes these days. We have to have a good team. We need to be able to rely on each other, in business, just like in the air."

NaTasha S. McNeil:

Lamar Advertising and Cute for Christ

NaTasha is a beautiful young lady with a passion for fashion and for God. Her faith is strong and she certainly loves style. She decided to create a clothing company that would allow ladies to be modest, while still feeling beautiful.

She explained our friendship, "I've adopted you, Dr. Shellie, as my mentor. You're just so fabulous! With all your hustle and bustle in life, you're able to still, give guidance, even through social media. It's really encouraging on a day-to-day basis to see positive statuses and just, boosts us in the right direction. Your posts push people to be the best them. I really do appreciate that, because so much of our time is occupied on social media, so what we do read on a day-to-day basis does matter, and so, thank you for that."

NaTasha read an article about an educational leader from a Catholic high school who had a group of 200 young girls that would come to school with their uniforms on, but they would roll their skirts up. Their blazers were pretty long, so they went over the short skirt, and so it looked as if they didn't have on any bottoms.

The administration had been telling the students and the parents, 'This is something that we're going to have to enforce. You can't do this, and these are the reasons why, based on the school's policy.' I read in the article, that what he ended up doing was, suspending 200 students from class that day because they all would not listen, and all of the girls kept rolling their skirts up.

It was discovered that 35 percent of those girls were really peer pressuring the other girls to do it, and some of them didn't even know what they were doing. They just thought, 'I want to be cool. I want to be in the in crowd. I want to look just like them, so, yeah, let me roll up my skirt too.' There is a lot of peer pressure to deal with when you're in the earlier ages of developing your identity.

"I remember we went to the Statehouse in Columbia, South Carolina, and there was another young lady that sang for the Senator there, who suggested, 'You know what? Act dignified,' and at the time, honestly, I didn't know what 'act dignified' meant. Once I discovered what that meant, I was able to project that image daily."

Natasha's mission and motto for her boutique is based on Proverbs 31:25, "She is clothed with strength and dignity; she can laugh at the days to come." Natasha believes style showcases our personalities, and modesty is a representation of self-appreciation.

NaTasha advised Empowering Women Radio listeners to, "Let your style, internally and externally show through. If your style is to smile even through the pain and with adversity, do it. If your style is to overcome it with kindness, let that speak for you. Show us who you truly are and let your style reflect that.

Nikole Li Aston:

Astonishing Style and Trends & Tresses

When collaboration works naturally, it is a beautiful thing. Women are buying, marketing together in droves and making an impact together. Nikole Li was the Stylist of the Year for Style Week, which is organized by the fabulous Wadria Taylor. Nikole also owns her own boutique, Trends & Tresses, which sells fabulous clothing and high quality hair products.

When Nikole styled me for an event recently, I absolutely loved that moment. I loved her boutique, and the clothing she chose showcased my style and personality. I explained to Nikole, that back in the day, I had a debate with a young new publicist. She looked at me and said "there is no way you're going to be able to be an inspiring woman in fancy Gucci shoes or Chanel outfit! We're going to have to put you in Birkenstocks and hippie clothes, so you can be taken seriously as a humble humanitarian."

I asked Nikole her take on this idea of branding based on stereotypes about how a person should dress. Nikole vehemently stated, "I completely disagree. I feel that everyone has their own individual style. You can tweak it, whether you dress it up or dress it down. Whatever you need to do to put your best foot forward or whatever works for you, I say go for it. I feel like whatever makes you shine or feel your best, just do it, and if it's a positive feeling you get from that, make it happen!"

Nikole explained, "Many women are in business these days empowering other women. We are spreading the positivity and sharing our visions while bringing other women up with them; helping another one out. I just love that feeling and vibe. I could never get enough of it. I just offer my experience and my services to uplift and help another woman in business, and just everybody work together to make everything great. That's what I stand for."

She has a great eye for detail, as well as what will work on a runway or a red carpet. She explained, "I like to bring out the best in my clients. I'm going to get what works for you, your body type, your personality and just basically turn you around and bring you back to life.

"I'm definitely for all shapes, all sizes. I believe that beauty comes in all forms, shapes and figures. So, I can definitely style from size 00 and all the way beyond. I think in making my clients feel comfortable in what they have on, and also getting them the proper fit, whether they are very tiny or on the plus size.

"The proper foundation is the first thing to start with an outfit, and that's what I highly recommend to all of my clients. Having the proper foundation will set off your entire outfit. So, for women especially, you'll want to make sure you have on the proper bottoms, make sure you have a proper fitting bra, and that's the basic foundation for any outfit. But, I feel like being a different size, whether it's being very small or very large fashion can accommodate all of those, and I definitely welcome any of my clients, all sizes to visit me and get together, get a style session going to help me pick out the best outfit for them."

Nikole mentioned, "A person's self-brand definitely comes from their personality and the type of person they are. I really like women to be empowered. I really want to bring out the best in other women. If they don't have a voice, I want to give them a voice. Give a lady a reason to be confident; to live out loud and be themselves. Really, it comes down to their personality, and just showcasing what they do or what they're talented at, or what they do best. I believe that having the proper look really brings that out. If you look good, you're going to feel great."

Empowering Women Radio asked for advice for a young woman who is just going down a new business path; on the flip side, for a woman who is a little older, who has children at home and is just starting an entrepreneurial venture but doesn't quite know how to make that leap. Nikole responded, "Coming from the corporate world, full-time 9-5 world, which I am definitely accustomed to… first, don't make excuses. There's no better time than the present. If you have a vision, and you have a dream, I definitely say go for it. I put mine off for quite a while, and I had my wake-up call and it just came to me in my vision and I made it happen. It wasn't an easy process, but nothing worth having is.

"Stay true to your vision, stay true to your ways and how you want things done. Stick up for yourself, stand your ground and just move forward. I definitely recommend a lot of research before jumping into anything, and definitely, find a very good mentor to help you every step of the way and assist you in bringing your vision to life.

"Definitely be you, be positive and love yourself 200%. If you don't love yourself, no one else is going to, so you have to love yourself first…put your best foot forward and let that be in Louboutins!"

Miyoshi Anderson:

iModel and Pittsburgh Fashion Week

Her beauty and poise are evident the instant she walks into the room. I recall practicing my chorography for the All That Jazz singing and dancing number for our Fabulous Forties event. All heads turned when Miyoshi Anderson entered the hotel banquet room to prepare for MCing fashion show. I heard someone whisper, "Who is that lovely model?" Miyoshi has even been described as a "unicorn" on social media videos because her beauty has such a unique wow factor.

Miyoshi Anderson is the Founder and CEO of both the iModel System & Pittsburgh Fashion Week. She explained to Empowering Women Radio how she created Pittsburgh Fashion Week, "It actually started with me as a model, and I had modeled for so long and for so many clients. Yet, during the beginning of the millennium, it started to dwindle, and so I found that to be a problem. Not just for myself, but also for my fellow friends who also modeled. As I researched and watched what was going on year after year, I thought, 'Well, could there actually be a fashion week here in Pittsburgh?'

"I am closely related to Fashion Week in New York, and during those times, I just continued to get inspired and think how can we improve and create more work and income for models, and this was the thought that came to me.

"In a matter of three and a half years, I started to write what a Fashion Week in Pittsburgh would look like. I studied the market in Pittsburgh, how things worked and what the needs here, were. We had the inaugural year September of 2010."

I had the opportunity to attend an iModel system of workshops led by Miyoshi. She explained, "The iModel system was created during the same time Pittsburgh Fashion Week was a thought up as well. I brought up what I had been doing for models during my time of modeling, and my business coach said, 'Miyoshi, you can create a system out of this.' I thought, that I never thought to create a system or a program. We started brainstorming and created a three-step system.

"The economy was shifting, and I was trying to create or figure out ways of creating more work and income for us frustrated models out there. What we came up with was a system that could do that, and I've seen it work because even before the iModel system was created, she said, 'Miyoshi, this system is already working for you because you're doing it.'

"My goal is to go out and encourage young adults of the ages of 13 to 17, and to also encourage those aspiring models and those professional models that may feel a little stuck in trying to move to the next level. Even the everyday woman or man, the everyday person, to help them kind of shape or reshape their lives.

"The bigger question that we pose to the participants is, 'What are you modeling after?' That's at the core of what iModel system is." I asked Miyoshi what she models herself after and she replied, "I model after integrity, definitely inspiration. I get inspired by other women, such as you, Dr. Shellie. I try to be a positive example and so those are the things that I model after."

The Fashion Hall of Fame event that Miyoshi holds annually in Pittsburgh is in a golden ballroom in the historic Omni William Penn. I had her explain why it's important to her to acknowledge and honor those in the fashion industry that she respects, to which she responded, "It is very near and dear to my heart and is one of the largest segments throughout Pittsburgh Fashion Week during the week.

"The reason why we decided to bring about such a concept was because these fashionistas, have impacted the city, particularly, Pittsburgh, with fashion, style and beauty. Much of our younger generation, don't know that about them and the impact that they have so bestowed here on the city. My point was to cross these two generations and to give acknowledgment of what these individuals have done here in the city.

"As the process begins, we send out a press release to the city asking for nomination requests. The individual must have at least ten years of experience in order to accept an award of such stature, and then once we have pulled those names, I am not one of those who look into, you know, who's been nominated. I wait until after the whole process is finished, because it would definitely be a conflict of interest.

"Once it's all said and done and I get the list of names, then we get to announce who will go into the induction. The event is at the Omni William Penn Hotel, which is one of the most luxurious hotels downtown and one of the oldest. I thought it would be such a fitting place of grandeur and elegance to honor these individuals who have impacted us with fashion, style and beauty."

Miyoshi's Pop Up C.O.R.E. is popping up all over social media. Miyoshi explained her video segments, "Pop Up Fashion C.O.R.E. is where I pop up to a fashionista's home, whether they are in the line of fashion, style, beauty, fitness or health, and I pop up at their establishment, and I interview them.

"The word Core, C.O.R.E., is an acronym that stands for Create Opportunity for Real Exposure, so when I pop up to interview them, it gives Pittsburgh Fashion Week a chance to show a continuum throughout the year with other fashion events. It also provides exposure to fashionistas here in the city, and I've also interviewed those in other parts of the country as well.

"It's just another way for fashion folks to enjoy a fashion event or to hear about someone that they had not heard about before. Get to know who they are, how they got started and how they can be contacted and supported."

Miyoshi is humble and yet beautiful. I asked her how we too, can have that type of internal confidence that shines outward. After thanking me for the compliment, Miyoshi said that, "The first word that comes to mind is love, and I do try to support this scripture, 'Perfect love casts out fear.'

"When you love humanity and love people and are genuinely concerned about their healthy minds and bodies it can be felt by others. You can model after those types of inspirations. I try to model after love because I'm genuinely interested in people, such as yourself.

"I think because I want to help people and they come to me with some of the things that they want to improve and want to bring out of them, we try to dig deep and figure out what those points are. We help them to work on those particular areas."

Miyoshi's iModel program teaches the students to soar with their strengths. She feels that often her guidance is needed, "Even to point out where their weaknesses are, because then we have to lean on other people who are stronger in those areas without being afraid to do so. That is sometimes a challenge."

Tips that Miyoshi has for us all collaborating and working together include; finding, "Women who are like-minded and who are at a point that you want to reach. Find women who are on the same playing field as you. You should share similar aspirations."

To Miyoshi, empowering other women means that, "There is a confidence within yourself to help other women and to also be helped, to lead and also be led. You encourage others, but also encourage yourself, and want to be encouraged. There is a freedom that has to happen within you. There is a confidence that exudes even when the woman doesn't feel their best. Certain days I don't feel my best, but that's when you learn go to talk to and encourage yourself. Sometimes going into prayer and meditation, just being in a quiet headspace to evaluate and to strengthen one's self is the way that I would go.

"Always find women who are just as encouraging as you are. There are times when we are around individuals (because of whatever life has thrown them) who aren't as encouraged and don't feel as positive. I'm around those individuals as well. I love having the grand opportunity to affirm that, 'You are beautiful. You have greatness within. You have potential. Come to a point where you can embrace all that you have to offer the world.'"

Chapter 8:

Pay it Forward

'I Am Malala' is a memoir that was written by the young girl activist who was shot in the head on the school bus by a member of the Taliban. Due to Malala Yousafzai's dedication to assuring that girls can be educated too in Pakistan, readers were taken on a journey to understand from her stand point why women empowerment and their education is so important. I have met many women who have turned their life stories into humanitarian movements and charitable works to pay it forward for those who have experienced the pain of what they themselves had been through.

Rose Morris:
Pay It Forward and the Safety Sleeper

Rose Morris is the President/Founder of Abrams Bed and the Director of Fund It Forward, which is a non-profit that provides resources for children with special needs. She invented the Safety Sleeper.

She explained how it all came to be by telling the story about her child who is on the autism spectrum, "Honestly, I say this without joking; it was by the grace of God that we had this bed. My son Abram was two; he was very smart and climbing out of his crib. We had something at home to keep him contained. He just wouldn't shut down; he was the 'energizer bunny'. Almost like he was obsessed with…if he could get out, he needed to get out, and so he stayed awake trying to do that. We tried to go on vacation and it was not very successful. It was frustrating to myself, to my husband, to the family we were staying with; so we came home.

"We tried again and the same thing happened. The third time we tried, we went to visit some friends who I had always called my 'surrogate family' in Dallas. We stayed with them and I said 'If Abram gets up, he can't sleep...there is nothing we can do to contain him; this is going to be a tricky week.' My friend there laughed and said 'Oh I can figure something out!' I said, 'Go ahead.' They devised something and sure enough about eleven o'clock Abram came running out across the hall. I just laughed at that point because I was like 'Yeah, he showed you!' That summer was torture for us as parents.

"The next day my friend Mark said, 'You know, we've got a shop' because they built boat covers. He explained, 'I think we can figure something out. What do you need?' I said, 'Well, it works at home because we have x, y and z. We have a crib that has a cover and he's in there; but we can't travel, for that there's nothing we can do.' Then I said, 'He's going to grow so I need something to be a twin size mattress.'

"My husband and Mark started talking, scheming things up. I tuned them out; I didn't really believe they were going to do anything. It was more like 'Put your money where your mouth is!' I wasn't ready to believe anymore that somebody could help me out.

"So that trip ended and we came home. Abram proceeded to then, get out of his crib. He put a hole in it. He got out and got into something, so I could tell he had gotten out. He got back in and was sitting there looking at me like, 'Yeah, I'll get out whenever I want!' I was just devastated.

"My husband was out of town, and I had a new baby; she was an infant, and I had an almost teenage child; I was just done. It was like 'What am I going to do with this child?' I called our friend and said, "Do you have that bed? Do you think you can make that for real? I really think I want you to give it a shot.' He said 'Oh. I've already got it done, I'll send it to you.' That was a huge relief!"

"We had this sleeping thing and I was just excited when we got this bed. To be able to put it out there to help someone else…I knew the feeling I felt when we got it. To be able to put it out there, and see if anybody else had the same problems, I did to see if this could help, there was no question; we would just do it.

"We took something that could be seen as a negative and turned it into a positive. It is similar to my experience with finding out he was on the spectrum. I was never disappointed when we got the autism diagnosis. I was relieved, because at least we knew what the problem was and we could tackle it, which we did, in our own way."

As a special education professor myself, I can totally understand the need for Fund it Forward resources. One of the stories that I heard Rose tell to my students at the university and at the women in a business event was the "Little Luke and the blue paint story". She tells the story, "Luke and his mom live in the Houston area. She's a single mom and has three kids (two girls and a boy). He was severely autistic. They had just moved into a new house and done what they needed to do. They put in new hardwood floors, they had painted, and it was all fresh and clean. One night Luke went to bed fairly early, about eleven as she recalls; she was excited. She was going to get a good night's sleep. Sometime at two or three in the morning, she heard him laugh and she was thinking 'Oh he's laughing!' Suddenly she realized, 'Why is he laughing at my door, it's two in the morning?'

"The mother got up and opened the door. Luke had gotten the blue paint out of the garage and was smearing it all over himself. He had poured it all over his head and all the way down his body, just really getting into the sensation of the sensory feeling that he was getting from that blue paint. Obviously, he was not happy when his mom yelled for the girls, and then came to try to get him into the bathroom.

"He then began flinging his arms and fighting them off. Imagine what happens when you fling an arm with blue paint all over it. The house was just covered in blue paint and just everything was such a mess! The new carpet, the new hardwood and the walls... because of course he was grabbing onto the walls as they were trying to get him into the bathroom and bathtub. Luke was not happy about getting rid of the blue paint. So kids like Luke and Abram really needed the Safety Sleeper."

Rose explained her non-profit organization, "Fund It Forward began because I started the business called Abrams Bed that sells an enclosed, portable bed for special needs kids. My son Abram needed that specific help, and I couldn't find anything out there for him. I felt the pull that I was supposed to put it out there for other people and try to help them.

"Basically the non-profit business just took off on its own, without me really knowing anything about business or how to run one or start one. What happened is that so many families would call me and just have such a serious need, but they would not have the means to pay for the Safety Sleeper. I felt like there had to be some help. So, we started the non-profit Fund It Forward to help. Initially, it was to get the bed, but almost as soon as we started it, we realized that it needed to be for more equipment.

"Fund It Forward helps families with special needs children obtain adaptive equipment that insurance usually don't cover. So have a wide variety of resources... from Safety Sleepers to iPads; communication devices to adaptive bicycles; a variety of things. We almost don't want to say no and that's kind of our motto; if you can tell us why you need it and how it's going to benefit the child, we will say yes that we'll help you and we go from there."

I talked to Rose about how she spreads the word to other moms and networks. Rose responded that, "A lot of it has just been me coming out of my comfort zone and talking about it. I'm nervous to talk too much about what I do because I don't want people to get tired of hearing me talk about it and tune me out.

"Every once in a while, somebody will give me a nugget and I'll grab onto it and say, 'Would you like to do more? Could you help me?' I put it out there that I need help through odd places such as social media. I ask friends and neighbors. I ask people like you at networking events. Also, friends of friends, people who hear about this story and believe in us, and talk to other people. Sometimes they come on board; prefer quality over quantity."

Rose talked about the transition process of becoming an entrepreneur, "I didn't know what I was going to do, or how I was going to do it, I'm an educator, I don't have any business background, but somehow this business has grown. I'm so fortunate. It's more of a passion; it's not a job, it's fun."

I said to Rose that I could relate to not feeling like a businessperson. No matter what I achieve in the entrepreneurial world, I still think of myself as a teacher first at my core.

Rose explained that to a new person wanting to start their own business, if it's not their original position or what they trained for, "If you've found something that you're passionate about, you can go anywhere with it, but, if you wanted to do something that you are not passionate about, I would say 'Step back and find your passion.'

"The first thing I would say is to reach out for help. Too often we don't ask for help when we need it. Find a mentor or find someone who has gone in a direction similar as you, or has some skill that you don't have, because I think it is smart to utilize the wisdom that is around us."

Jacquelyn Aluotto:
NIMBY Project and Real Beauty Real Women

Jacquelyn Aluotto and I share a love for working with homeless women and children. I traveled to New York to be filmed for a trailer for her NIMBY media project. Her energy was contagious and the celebrities that she had chosen for the public service announcement were wonderful. In was great to bond over a common love of serving the needs of those who are in housing transition.

Jacquelyn Aluotto explained to Empowering Women Radio how she began this giving back journey, "I was driving my car and I heard a radio personality state, 'Every nine seconds in America, a woman is beaten...' I listened to them explain how many homeless children there are in here fleeing abuse and I wanted to show what it was really like to be a battered woman in America.

"I was young. I decided I was going to go out and make a difference, and really film how homeless, battered women and children live across America. I knew that I needed filming equipment and travel money, so I saved, over a couple years, more than $20,000 in quarters. It was a very unconventional way to save money, but I had always worked in a restaurant, and I would make all of this money in change. I just became really active and just saved everything in change and money, and I started putting dollar bills in those big spring bottles, and in a couple of years I had saved $20,000.

I bought a bunch of film equipment and hired some people, and we made the first documentary, 'Not In My Backyard'. That was just the beginning of everything, to really show how battered women and their children flee abuse in America, and live in shelters. Yes, it was all funded with quarters."

She feels that, "You really can truly do anything. I know sometimes that when you're in the middle of it, it can seem impossible, but you really can do anything. I did not have resources. I did not come from a wealthy family. I didn't have the proper education to be making the films I'm doing, fund a non-profit, or run a pledge campaign. I did it, and all I say to people is 'if you're disciplined and you come up with a plan, stick with it. No one can see what you see through your eyes, and if you believe in your heart that you can make it work, go after it and do it."

Jacquelyn started another successful women-centered project. She explained, "Americans love beauty, glamour and entertainment. They love celebrities. They love fashion, and they just really love the glitz and the glamour. I created Real Beauty Real Women (RBRW) because I wanted to make activism sexy, so I started pairing celebrities with causes, and we created the show. It's kind of, Access Hollywood with a cause where I interview celebrities, and they talk to me about their non-profits or charities, and then they take me and the cameras into their red carpet events."

She recalled starting in New Jersey and New York with the hands-on makeovers of the women in SOS Shelter for battered women, "We ended up making over 48 women. They got a makeover from head to toe, and they did a fashion show. The fashion show was presented to the community starring the women and the children.

There's such a stigma with people that live in shelters, and we wanted to show that no one is really that different. It ended up turning out to be such a beautiful day. It really was amazing and we were really blessed that we got a lot of press, and we had so many celebrity stylists that really came out and did an amazing job and just so many volunteers. We are very lucky that Real Beauty Real Women has really just taken off from there."

Another cause, that Jacquelyn is a public advocate for is that, "Sexual trafficking needs to be brought to the forefront. We need to discuss how you can spot a predator or spot when someone is trafficking a child, and whether it's on an airplane, or if they're just walking in the mall; but it is a quiet epidemic and it is happening everywhere. On one of our shows, we talk about the Red Light Children's District. It really is a big global issue.

"It also is a very profitable issue because so many people are making money off of trafficking. I think that is another reason why it's happening on such a large scale.

"There are so many different shelters that handle sexual trafficking, Red Light Children, we've worked with. In New York City, we're working with the Good Shepherd. A lot of the children, they haven't been trafficked, but they've been sexually exploited. We really need to really get cracking, change laws and really educate people in their neighborhoods.

"There are over a hundred thousand children and young women who are trafficked in America. We really need to address this. We do not want our children trafficked in this country, or out of this country, and it really does start with changing laws."

One modern way to be an activist is to partner with companies that are taking on causes, and utilize their resources, "Businesses should partner with organizations and the leaders in the non-profit world. Consumers really are seeking out socially-conscious companies. We really are evolving as people, and we're saying, 'Huh, those are the same two hats, and if 20% of this hat is going to help end poverty, of course that's the hat I am going to buy.'

"Cause marketing is important. There are billions of dollars consumers will spend; yet, now they will only buy products that are giving back and are socially conscious.

"I do see this shift towards giving back and I love it. I'm excited about it, because it's just a great way to really make a difference. It's also a really good way for a filmmaker, like myself, to partner and obtain proper funding so that I can continue to go out and get sponsors. With the right support and funding, we can create amazing films. We want to impact people's lives and make a positive change."

Dr. Roli Chauhan:
Medical Doctor and Entrepreneur

Dr. Roli and I have attended many cause/fashion related red carpet events together in New York City. We were featured guests at Global Sisterhood of Empowering Women's member, Jyoti Soni's Mover and Shakers awards. We do these things in collaboration because we both love getting glammed up, but we also love giving back.

When I interviewed her for a segment on Inspiring Lives with Dr. Shellie, she spoke about the dowry brides in her homeland of India. It is on her heart to make an impact on this cultural concern. Dr. Roli explained on Empowering Women Radio, "This is a very serious issue and I do not want to say anything negative about my home country India, because I am proud of being an Indian origin woman; yet, I'm going to address this. Dowry is a social evil, not a normal thing in society.

"A dowry is a practice where the bride brings a gift to the groom and his family at the time of the wedding. This is one thing that has plagued the culture. A lot of people don't want a female child because of this. The parents have to pay for her wedding when she grows up.

"They suffer because they cannot bring in dowry and the grooms, and their families demand lavish weddings; it's always expected, how much the bride can bring at the time of the wedding. I dealt with it on a personal level and got to experience it myself. Many women that I dealt with in my medical training saw first-hand the effects of it.

"A lot of women are harassed, tortured and I don't want to say this… but some are burned alive; I'm shaking as I'm speaking about it. I saw a lot of really visually graphic scenes at the hospital when I worked there.

"Women would be brought into the ER, with burns wrapped in blankets, and we would have to treat them in the ER. I was exposed to so much in the surgery ward. I had to do surgical dressings. When the men burnt victims, they all came in with the same made up story along the lines of the stove catching on fire.

"I could see it in the ladies' faces. What they were going through in their homes was not easy. They were hurting inside and out; a lot of times they lost their life.

"I saw the effects in other departments as well, like OB/GYN and other departments of the hospital. People just did not want a female child. Sometimes they would leave their child; babies were abandoned at the hospital, which was not a pretty scene. I dealt with a lot of graphic and unthinkable things over there. A lot of these social evils are hidden. It's all part of the mindset I believe.

"The male child is very important. They don't consider the family complete unless they have a baby boy. They celebrate the birth of the baby boy in that culture.

"I don't want to talk negatively. India is a powerful country; they have many powerful women; it's a land of power. Yet, I got to see gender issues in different forms, for example, some women did not know how to write their names in their own language. They simply aren't given that kind of importance, in some families.

"I'm not saying that this is 'the norm' in India; it's definitely not 'the norm'. It's just that I got to experience it first hand; I was the one dressing those patients surgically. I cannot forget the scenes.

"Once they get rid of this dowry problem, I think it will fix all the other female problems I have seen. Brides would no longer be burned, female infanticide would stop taking place, and fewer babies will be abandoned. Females will know how to write their names and obtain education. I sense that everything will fix up. Just get rid of the dowry problem; that's my only request to the Indian culture.

"Otherwise, I love being an Indian; I'm proud of being a woman of Indian origin; however, I'm happier in America just because of an incident that happened to me that had to do with dowry. The situation caused me to not be married.

"An empowered woman goes with what her heart wants. Don't be afraid of the world. Don't be submissive. Certainly, don't tolerate such injustice just because the culture tells you to be submissive and not speak up.

"If the culture labels you as bad because you aren't married, don't give in to that. You are born, unique yourself. You are here on this earth as a special unique person. Don't be afraid to be who you are!"

Kelly Wallace Ventricle:

Kelly's Kollections Boutique

Kelly Wallace is a sassy business owner of a boutique in her small hometown. After she styled me for multiple events, Kelly put her fashions on the runways of the Fabulous Forties fundraiser. Because of business owners like her, it all came together so that we could raise over $100,000 for the Homeless Children's Education Fund.

Kelly explained, "Dr. Shellie really taught me a lot about how the Fabulous Forties was going to work. She asked me to be in it like months before, and I was a little bit nervous, but you know what? She made me feel at ease and relaxed. I liked when the models came in and we got to dress them. It was fun collaborating with vintage and vogue styles. I really loved doing it."

She hasn't always been a business owner. Kelly said, "I was a single mother. I have a daughter, Dominica, who is now 22. I was used to it being just the two of us for a long time as I was working my jobs. It's a day-by-day learning process. I'm getting to know every aspect and angle of being a small business owner.

"From waxing the floors to doing the merchandising and the budget, it can be hard to do it and learn it all, especially if you didn't get an MBA; it is hard to do the budgets and the numbers." She admitted, "It can be very trying. I sometimes tend to get down on myself, but then I bring myself back up. I say, 'I can do this. I can do this, and I love it. I enjoy it.' I recommend if someone has a dream or a goal in their life, they should go with it."

We talked about supporting non-profits with talents, "I always feel better doing something for a charity. There's so much sadness in this world today that I feel we need to help in any way that we can. I like to do charity work with a range of causes, from the elderly to autism."

Many businesswomen these days are developing giving back strategies as a part of their business plans. They are tapping into what they love and what they want to support. Kelly stated that, "A lot of people, back in the day, had businesses only to make money. I think it's rewarding at the end of the day to do something for charity, to give back."

Kelly told Empowering Women Radio why it is important to pay it forward, "It's not all about money and glamour; It's about doing something kind for someone once a day, and you should do something (such as a kind word or opening a door).

"Once a day, I try to pay it forward, by at last giving a true compliment, or with the little ladies at drugstore up the street, I'll carry their groceries and help get bags in the car. I have a lot of elderly ladies that come in to the shop and I tell them to sit down and rest, and I'll get them a soda or bottle of water. You should pay it forward with everything. The movie Pay It Forward, with Kevin Spacey and Helen Hunt, it really made an impact on me when I watched it. That is now a big motto of mine, 'pay it forward'.

"Remember, if you have a dream or a goal inside you and you're afraid to do it… Don't be afraid. You've just got to go with your heart, peace of mind and just move forward. Try not to have negativity in your life. Be positive, pray. I pray to God. That's my savior.

"Go for your goals and dreams, because if you don't, you're just going to say, 'I could have did this, I would have did this'. The key to success is you've got to follow your heart. Just go forth with it."

Chapter 9:

Family

My children are my world. When I look at my son's dimples when he grins, and hear my daughter talk about wanting to change the world; my heart melts.

I was blessed to find Dr. Kenneth Judson who my darling children call "Mr. Ken". We were married recently and he took on my children as his own. I love that my family feels complete and my soul feels at peace. I am so grateful for his friendship and love.

Family has always been important to me. My greatest role models are my parents Dr. and Mrs. Jack and Libby Jacobs. They taught me about incredible work ethic, giving back to society and they were my first examples of true unconditional love.

Dr. Patsy Torres Lucero:

The Positive Choice Tour

Dr. Judy Staveley, the creator of The Platform Magazine, introduced me to the fabulous Dr. Patsy Torres Lucero. It was wonderful to speak with this Latin singer. She spoke with Empowering Women Radio about how her Positive Choice Tour came to be. "Because I'm a performer, singer and I had a full band with dancers and musicians, I started speaking at schools for kids. Due to my education, and they started inviting me for career days where I would talk to the kids because I was known as a singer in my hometown of San Antonio, Texas.

"The kids would always ask me to sing, and, of course, I would just sing something a cappella or a teacher would pull out a guitar and go 'Bling, bling, bling, okay, do you know La Bamba?' out of tune.

"At one point, I said, 'You know, it would be really neat if I could actually bring my band and perform for the kids.

Give them my messages, but mix it with music.' The high school that I graduated from, they said, 'Well, let's try it here!' The kids responded so fantastically.

"We started touring schools. I ended up giving it a name and calling it The Positive Force Tour. This was just at high schools, because everyone said that, 'Oh, high school kids are too old and it's too late for them.' Everybody was always visiting elementary schools and maybe a middle school, but always overlooking the high schools. The Positive Choice Tour was going into high schools and telling students, 'Stay away from drugs, quit drugs, get out of gangs, stay in school, go on for higher education.' The nay-sayers said, 'Oh, they're not going to listen,' but these kids listened!

"It was awesome. One of the kids in Texas in a little-bitty town, little south Texas town called Clara, and this boy saw me there. He said he was inspired so much that he went on, and he got a scholarship and went on to Harvard. One day, I received a phone call from the president of the Hispanic Society at Harvard. He was the high school kid from Texas. He explained that he could have gone just any way with his life, but he just said it was the inspiration seeing a Latino doing it. It let him know that he could achieve as well.

"My father is Mexican and my mother is American (of German, Irish and Scottish decent). They met in Japan when they were both in the army. That is where they made me, so we always joke I was 'Made in Japan'.

"Then they came home, and I was born in San Antonio, Texas. I've always embraced the Latino culture. Spanish was never spoken in the house. My father was trying to learn English, so he always spoke English. So, I learned Spanish later, in high school and college. I am so intrigued with all kinds of cultures and the Mexican culture; it's our sister country right there. There's so much with the food, the traditions. Family is such a strong part of the Hispanic culture, and our family is very, very strong. That's a beautiful part of it; the music is a lovely part of it also.

"I am proud of my American heritage and my Mexican heritage. That's what makes me... me.

"I think of an empowered woman as a woman that doesn't see barriers, that sees opportunities; that when I'm challenged with something, even if it scares me to where I feel those butterflies in my stomach, like 'can I do this?' and then I think, 'You know what, I'm not going to know unless I try,' because sometimes something in you might say, "I can't do it," or it might say, 'Well, maybe later. Let me practice more or let me get more experience,' but I said, 'No, you know, the opportunity is here and now. I'm just going to do my very best.'

"If it doesn't work out, hey, I'll get better and I'll learn, but I'm not going to pass up an opportunity. I'm not going to let there be barriers, because we have enough barriers as women, so don't put up your own barriers. You've got to go out there and go for it."

I asked, Patsy what opportunity she grasped that she was thankful that she did, and she replied, "I would say that was the opportunity to go back to school, because originally, my grandfather from Mexico was a doctor, a medical doctor, and I just loved him. He inspired me. Since

I was five years old, I wanted to be Dr. Torres like him, and I saw how the patients loved him. He loved what he did; his hands were healing hands.

"My grandfather was a general practitioner; he did everything. He did surgery; he delivered babies. It was back in the day when doctors did everything. My grandfather was just amazing.

"I grew up saying, 'That's what I'm going to do.' All through high school, I was getting ready for pre-med, and suddenly, my little sister decided that she wanted to play the saxophone and get in the marching band. I saw her getting out of class all the time. I decided, 'I want to get out of class too,' so I picked up the trumpet, started playing trumpet just to get out of class and go on field trips.

"That prompted us putting together a little group, and I got really good at playing trumpet. She was really good at playing sax, and we made a little popular dance band. After high school graduation, when we started college, the group expanded more. The band talked me into starting to sing just a little bit, because my sister went off and got married, and the next thing you know, I got discovered within six months from my singing.

"They put me on a record to record what's called Tejano music; Tejano music is a regional music here in Texas. It's a blend of the Mexican music with almost a hybrid of country and jazz, if you can think of that, because the chords are almost jazz-oriented, but the beat is kind of faster, like a country beat, and the words are Spanish.

"I got a recording contract, doing Tejano music, and then suddenly I was associated with it, and I'm 'Patsy

Torres, Tejano singer and artist'. I kept saying, 'No, I'm Patsy Torres, the trumpet player that's going to be a doctor.'

"It was like a whirlwind. I started getting all kinds of opportunities. I got tours, I got on magazines, I got record deals, I got sponsorships; everything was going great, but I kept thinking... 'when are they going to figure out I'm not a real singer?'

"I was going to college, and it was very hard at that time, because I was talking about inorganic chemistry class at 7:30 in the morning, and I had just gotten in at 4:00 in the morning from my show the night before. When I graduated with my science degree, I felt like I had to make a decision. I couldn't do both anymore. I wasn't doing justice to either one because I was so exhausted, so I went to my grandfather, Dr. Torres, and I sat there with him and said, 'Now that I've graduated, it's time to get serious,' and he said, 'Yes.' I said, 'I can't do both anymore.'

"He said, 'No, you can't. Nieta, you have a God-given gift. You need to sing.' I couldn't believe it. If he had told me, 'Okay, buckle down; go to school,' I was going to quit right then.

"I didn't need to keep singing, but at that point, I was already doing my little talks at schools and helping kids. After my talk with my grandfather, I just took off. I made The Positive Force Tour, recorded more albums and I was just touring all over.

"I reached probably a million kids or more, getting these wonderful letters from kids, you know, about changing their lives, and then I incorporated The Positive

Force Tour and made other programs for middle schools, elementary schools, different age groups and I started feeling a little empty.

"I started saying, 'Am I just going through the motions now? I mean, I'm so busy and I'm doing so much,' Then I got a phone call, and they said, 'Can you do some promos for the university here in town, but we can only pay you with semester, not money?'

"I said, 'Yeah, I'll do that, take a couple courses.' My mind was hungry, and I did. I made two A's, and they said, 'How would you like to get a degree here? We will give you a scholarship for a degree. Just promote our university and sing for us whenever we want you to sing,' so I did.

"It was a blessing. That's when you know it's God-sent. Look at all the students now that have all these giant student loans over them, but if that wasn't enough, I got a master's in education with them. I graduated distinguished with a 4.0, and they said, 'Patsy, would you like to keep going for your Ph.D.?'

"It was funny. They offered me a scholarship for my Ph.D. and I thought, 'Well, what do I need a Ph.D. for? I'm a professional performer, singer. I tour all over. I've gone overseas.' I had just been in Turkey and I did an Asian and European tour, but when you get offered something like that, I said, 'This is Heaven-sent.' God wanted me to learn.

"Education changes you. It changes your perspective on yourself, on your environment, and on others. Remember Plato, the fact that the ones that learn, the philosophers, we're supposed to turn around and lead the other ones out of the dark. We're supposed to enlighten other people with what we learn, with our knowledge. We're supposed to pass on wisdom.

"When I started telling people, 'Well, I guess I'm going to go for my Ph.D.,' I was surprised how many people said, 'Why? Oh, that's going to be so long. I mean how long will it take?' I would say, 'Well, five to ten years.' They replied with, 'Are you kidding? That's just ridiculous.'

"I said, 'You know what, in five years, either I can just be older or I can have my doctorate.' They were offering me a degree. How can I just leave that? I was a little scared wondering if I could achieve it.

"Well, I went for it. I passed the admissions tests. I started doing my courses, and I just loved it, getting ready for my dissertation. Then just like a year before I was getting ready, finishing up my dissertation, one of my classmates said, 'What's it going to feel like when they call you Dr. Torres?'

"I realized then my dream came true. Dr. Torres like my grandfather; I couldn't believe it. God knew what would really make me happy in my heart. I mean, look at doctors these days. How often do they get to really spend time with patients? I'm a real people person.

"I recalled my grandfather saying to me, 'Be a healer of the soul, do preventative medicine,' and that's what I do when I use my music and my singing and reaching the kids (actually all ages now), by speaking and singing at the same events.

"I love it. I love meeting people. I love hearing their stories.

"I want to remind the ladies out there that we do have the power. I actually did a paper in my master's titled, 'Educate a Girl and Change the World,' because a woman, as the mother figure and usually the one that runs a household, she makes the difference. If she decides our family is going to go to church, get an education, help others or volunteer, usually that whole family unit does it, but the women are the leaders.

"We are leaders. We can change the world, and it's just a matter of empowering ourselves. I love to live by a quote by Gandhi. He said, 'Live life as if you were going to die tomorrow.' He said, 'Learn as if you're going to live forever.'

"I always say whatever you're doing; always do your very, very best. If you're mopping a floor, you mop that floor so good and so shiny that people say, 'Who mopped that floor? I've never seen it look that good.' Because whatever you do, just do your best. God will do the rest."

Mani Kamboj:

ARC Movie Productions, and Kamtiel Software

Mani Kamboj, lives in NY, but she grew up and did her Master's Degree and schooling in India. She is the president and co-partner of the Roshni Media group. She also runs New ARC Productions and Kamtiel Software company. Mani has done some modeling and she's even doing some Hollywood producing! Her beauty is stunning and her business acumen and love for family is wonderful.

Mani explained The Roshni Media Group, "It was founded by Dr. Roshni. I'm a big fan of her and the work she has been doing to give back to communities. They reached out to me because they wanted to feature me as an author. This is how I actually met her. We found some synergy to work together philanthropically. Roshni Media at that time was looking to go multiple platform you know, they wanted to release their books not only digitally, they wanted to do awards and different things they had in the pipeline. This was my forte and I have worked on media groups before also under Kamtiel Software. We put my energy and my skills to work for the company. I'm a partner now.

"The media group is focused on giving back to society. We support a lot of non-profit organizations under our umbrella, so this is more about working for others. That is an important value for us, and the people who support us. This is a people oriented media company.

"I started back in India at a technology company at the age of 23 years old as I got out of my master's program. In India, many people came forward to help me out when I was launching my firm. When women support each other, we empower the world.

"Deep inside my heart, and when I came to US a couple of years ago, I wanted to do things for others. So, when I started working with Roshni Media, www.roshnimedia.com; I realized it was the platform I could use to give back more. Roshni Media began to focus on those who have who have given back to our community. We make them stars. Through our media, we let people know about their missions and they can learn from their life.

"The Miss Universe pageant is a part of the Kamtiel Technology Company that I partner with my husband. When I started my company in India at 23 years old, I was even featured in a couple magazines for being a young entrepreneur back in India. That technology company works with developing all the web operations with a variety of clients: financial institutions, non-profit and media companies. So, when my company merged with my husband's company, he brought the Miss Universe Corporation as a client, so we take care of all of their web operations. When you see Miss Universe.com or Miss Teen USA, it is all our work because we manage their sites.

"Honestly, so far, I've never had an obstacle; in fact people are very supportive. Remember, I mentioned that people really came forward to support me when I launched my company. I never had an issue because I've always believed in one thing; if you can empower yourself, you really don't need to go out and seek support from others.

"Educate yourself with knowledge so that you can work towards empowering yourself. You don't really need to constantly seek help. I never really had to depend on anybody else. I was quite independent and have been really successful working that way.

"Trust me, both my husband and I work really hard. Running my technology company, I get the benefit that I can work from home, so I can look after my daughter. Definitely when you are a mother, you have your responsibilities. I do that, undoubtedly. I am wherever I am needed, at the playground and play dates, I am there and she is my highest priority. So this is where we balance our life and work. My husband has really been supportive and he has said that whenever you feel that you want to play your mother card, I am your help. You don't have to worry about that.

"My daughter wants to be in a leadership role; she is a very loving kid and a very peaceful soul. I can see that. Not really bragging about it, but she is a very content girl. She is a supportive child; she is watching me. I see that.

"Keep yourself updated with all the information that is available all around the world; you don't have to go far East or far West, but definitely you must try to look forward to what's happening in the future in that particular field. So, current information is very important.

"Stay on schedule: planning, planning and planning. This always keeps me going and moving straight ahead. For example, if you have a couple of meetings, you can always strategize it. Determine how much time you are going to invest in it. Figure out what information you will need to work on a project.

"Definitely, you need to prioritize your life. Your personal life and work balance, is the key factor. As I said, I enjoy spending time with my daughter, because that's what my highest priority is. Whatever you have made your highest priority, stick to it.

"If you think that your personal life is of utmost importance, then focus more of your energy on that. Whatever time you have left, throw into your fashion style or the work that you have.

"When your main priority is work…focus toward work, invest that kind of time and bring the balance to work with weekends with your family. Do things for them during the weekends; It is a balance that you will have to figure out for yourself.

"Also, try to give back. Trust me it's a Law of Attraction. The more you give, the more it comes back:

whether it's love, money, affection… whatever you give, it definitely comes back.

"It's about your own reflection. The way you are, it will come back to you. It's in your path. For example, when I am very happy, I am happy around people, it triggers happiness in others.

"This is what is Law of Attraction is. The way you are, the way you talk, the way you move… it will come back to you. If you are angry, it will come back to you with anger only. So it's basically to work on one's self only. I'm a very self-philosophical person and I try to be practical. They are the rules I always follow.

"I keep myself in a timetable, I try to balance my life, I try to plan before I get into a project and give back. Those are the simple rules.

"I would like to reach out to all those women who have things in their heart and want to speak out to the world about it. I would say, 'Come forward. Speak out. Talk to people: your neighbor or your best friend. Talk about it; it's not just your problem.

"Success and grief have to be talked about and shared. Discuss the good parts and the bad parts. I feel that a woman has the power to control and really lead her life in the way that she can. This is the biggest gift a woman has. So just do it, go talk."

Jen Forsyth:

The Happier Autism Family

Jen Forsyth was the President of a non-profit, but most importantly, she is a mother who meets the needs of her children even through the struggles of autism. Because I was a teacher, an assistant principal of students on the autism spectrum, and have been a special education professor for the last decade, our radio podcast discussed the trials, tribulations and successes of a mother autism advocate.

Jen is a friend who I would be up with to chat about her non-profit work; while our kids would run around places like Chuck E. Cheese. Her ability to focus on her non-profit changed dramatically recently and has shifted to getting her well again and her family.

You see, after the Empowering Women Radio interview... Jen began to get really sick. She explained to me the lowest point, "It was waking up with my second feeding tube. I had gone to a hospital for a second opinion. I was assured that they were going to help me. I woke up from my procedure in some of the worst pain in my life. The pain shot through my body and continued to get worse through the next several days. I cried, screamed, begged for relief. I looked into doctors' eyes pleading, 'Help me!' My pleas fell on deaf ears.

"Nothing could be immediately found on x-rays or scans, so they accused me of 'drug seeking' and actually withheld medications that would have made me feel better at times, or they gave me the bare minimum. Upon my discharge, one resident told me I should really check with a therapist because my 'pancreatitis,' in his opinion, was all in my head.

"I went to these people for help and left humiliated and more broken than when I entered. Thankfully, my wonderful family doctor shook me out of my depression and told me to get to the Cleveland Clinic as fast as I could be transferred.

"It turned out the feeding tube was placed on a live nerve, which was causing a great deal of the pain. I also had a severe staph infection, which was missed in a follow-up emergency room visit.

"I wasn't a drug seeker. It wasn't all in my head and my pancreatitis was indeed real, and my treatment got much better once I got to Cleveland.

"Through this journey, I am still so blessed! I have the best husband who will do anything for me, and three amazing children who have been so strong. We have also built up a community of friends who have been such a lifeline of support. People have done everything from send gift cards and meals, to just send me silly pictures of cats on Facebook. It all means the same to me. I feel the same amount of love and support from each gesture.

"People who were strangers or who weren't very close are now dear family friends. They say in times of crisis you find out who your real friends are. I have been very fortunate to find so many people are in my corner. They pick me up in my dark moments, they keep me going when I want to quit, they answer each and every call for help; I am never going to be able to repay all of this generosity. I just hope to pay forward in some way, when I am able to.

"'The Forsyth Five,' that's what we call ourselves now. We stick together and we do our best to communicate and help each other through. Our situation is definitely not easy right now. I am critically ill. Three children are affected here, including one who is pretty far down the autism spectrum.

"Nearly all of the family responsibilities have fallen to my husband, which is quite a burden. He must work, take care of the house, and then run kids to hockey, Miracle League, cheer, and any other practices and appointments that arise. This is also where our wonderful community of friends comes into play. Bless them all for helping so much! For the five of us: prayer, constant communication and cutting out drama have been the best things we have done.

"We hold close to our church and regularly invite our Pastor to the hospital to pray with us. Our community pitched in to care for our children when we needed help.

"We started having regular family meetings to

communicate and catch up with each other. At the end of each meeting, we pray together.

"No matter how many times I was in the hospital or how crazy things got, we had a sense of comfort, peace and togetherness. We all know we are there for each other, and that's how we get through the day.

"I learned to stand up for myself and demand the best care. I have a real illness, and I deserve proper treatment. I had no idea there was such a thing as an 'invisible illness' where you look okay, and you even have decent looking labs, but you are still seriously ill.

"Some doctors and nurses may not be educated on your particular condition and can say hurtful things to you. It happens in hospitals every day. Granted there are people who are addicts that do take advantage of the system, but some medical staff have become so jaded that they can be cruel to those who are really sick and really in need. That needs to change.

"The love and support I have been shown, from friends I already had to total strangers who have never met my family, has been truly overwhelming. God is so good to have put these people in my life. I don't believe in the worst in others. I believe in the very best, especially after this dark time in my life. I don't complain much even though things are bad. How can I, when I have so much love and support and so many people willing to help me? They are the reason I can stay so positive. As bad as things are, I feel blessed, protected and loved by so many.

"I look back on these past five years of my life. I have found out two out of three of my children were on the autism spectrum. I have moved three times, including one time where my family was thrown out by text, by a bad landlord and we had 25 days to find a new home. I had to fight two school districts to get proper autism care and education for my younger son. I had to fundraise and fight to get him a service dog, and that fight became a national battle in the media.

"I could have easily crawled into a hole and given up a long time ago. I could let things overwhelm me. I could have low self-worth. I chose to stand up and fight to make things right for others and myself.

"I will always see the good in the world, the good in others and the good in myself. I encourage other women to do the same no matter what the situation.

"It's my passion to help anyone who needs it with advice, resources or even just a caring ear to listen. After I am well again, my next venture is to begin writing a book with the working title of *The Happier Autism Family*. I plan to speak to families all over the world living with individuals on the autism spectrum. I want to showcase not only how to survive, but how to thrive. My goal is to bring hope and happiness to all families, and to get us to all to listen and understand each other."

Alice Beckett-Rumberger:
Therafusion

Alice Beckett-Rumberger is one of my dearest friends on earth. She was actually the first phone call I made when my former marriage was falling apart. She had been at this tipping point in her own life, with five children years ago. So I knew she would know the right words to say and steps to take. I am forever grateful for her friendship and guidance.

Alice is an amazing mother, grandmother and businesswoman. She explained, "I have worked for 25 years as a physical therapist. I graduated from the University of Pittsburgh, had some fantastic colleagues and had an opportunity to work in Philadelphia with professional athletes. It was a fantastic organization there and then I came back to Pittsburgh and reconnected with my friends in the professional community as a physical therapist.

"I've had a great opportunity to work, from professional athletes to infants, to everything in between, including the weekend warrior. I thought… I love this. While I loved it, I noticed a disturbing trend. The children who were coming to me were getting injured younger and younger. It seemed that they were getting injured doing things like sports without proper warm ups or stretching.

"I was running one day and I realized that there is this fusion between proper exercise and being able to teach those skills to kiddos. They needed body awareness so they wouldn't continue to get injured, so I came up with this idea of Therafusion, being physical therapy and injury prevention to kids.

"That grew into one segment, which morphed through a connection, with a client that I had into the corporate world. My company Therafusion began to work with different populations from corporation that needed their employees to discover fitness and wellness through education."

Beyond the business world, Alice's mothering and networking skills wowed me. She explained, "I have seven children, since I had two more after I remarried. It is an extreme blessing that we're able to live the life we have here in the United States. I've seen lives in other countries. That is exactly why we should help because we do have the blessings. We do have the opportunities to help kids. They are our future, and they need to know that we care."

Alice has forayed into my life in many ways. One way was through Gertrude Matshe, who is a woman who served as the International Rooney Scholar at Robert

Morris. I co-taught with Getrude at the university, but my story with her goes back a few years. She is the president of the Africa Alive Education Foundation, and we first connected when I was bringing the 'Luv my Woobie ® Blankets' initiative into the Pittsburgh shelters. Luv my Woobie blankets are high-end, beautiful blankets. For each blanket sold, my daughter and I would take another blanket to a local shelter, or Gertrude would take them to the AIDS orphans in Africa. Throughout the world, these beautiful blankets spread joy and warmth to children in need.

Alice recalled meeting Getrude, "That was really a fantastic evening. I completely remember that night when we all went out to dinner after you wrapped up taping 'Inspiring Lives with Dr. Shellie'. We were all out to dinner with the Camara sisters from Guinea and with Gertrude from Zimbabwe, and there was a connection that night among all of us. We were mothers, daughters or sisters. There was just a complete connection between all of us.

"Gertrude and I connected in particular, and she's a mother of three children. She's had to leave a country that she's from to start a new life somewhere so she can better help other people from her own country of origin, and I understand that, because we moved to the States. While we didn't have to flee to the States, we were always connected with my family in South America, and that was really an important connection in my life.

"She and I formed this fantastic friendship. I thought, here in Pittsburgh, we have needs and organizations and we have people here affected with AIDS; I had the wonderful opportunity to connect her with Kezia Ellison who educates teens about HIV and AIDS. Kezia has an office that does this here in the City of Pittsburgh."

Kezia is an amazing resource. She came in and spoke to my university students who are future teachers, as well. What an amazing young woman!

Alice explained, "It's working through those connections that I realized we could raise awareness about things that are happening here in our city and also things that are happening abroad because, some of the stuff is not very far away from us. While some of it is far, we are all human and we are all affected by it.

"I had a nice open house dinner at my home and we had people in to connect about AIDS in Africa and about other charities that I feel are important. Those kinds of connections seem to spread over and over and over again, so I think it's like planting a seed, and that seed grows. As Shellie says, they are 'Moving towards being empowered'. They realize, I have a gift and I can use my gift. Whatever that gift is, you find it, and you use it, and that is one of the important bridges between inspiring and empowering.

"I think that one of the biggest connectors between Shellie and myself, is that we are able to say, 'Hey, I can find the strength in this girl or woman'. It's not just women because I have sons, and I want my sons to be as compassionate as my daughters, too. We all really live in this world together, and we have to work to get along together."

Alice talked about the importance of friendship, "You know, that's just such a key thing because that is genuine, honest. You can have your girlfriends that you can talk to about things, and then you kind of walk away going, 'Wow, I feel good now. I feel recharged now about, the next things on our schedule.

"I deeply value my friendship with Shellie. We've been at the homeless children's center together, working with those kids, understanding the blessings that we have with our own children, and sometimes it's like, okay, we're not just moms. We're also professional women, too, and we can validate each other. I think through the partnerships, being the Health and Wellness Expert on her television show, we're able to do that so we have this great friendship and this great professional relationship, and it just promotes so much growth that it's very important to me."

I just had to ask Alice how she runs a household with a husband and a wife and seven kids and everybody is all different ages and going in different directions. Alice explained, "I think the first thing is communication, because I have big kids, older kids, teenage kids, kids out of college, that are living at home and putting themselves in a good career path; I want to help out as much as possible.

"The first thing is we have a really great family that communicates. We are always asking, 'Hey, what are you doing? What are you up to today or this week?' We have a schedule that the kids write down, when they're working, when they have practices and I try to fill in the blanks with the little ones, and what their schedule looks like.

"If I have to be somewhere, it's great, because I'll have an older daughter that will say, 'Okay, I have the kids during this time while mom has to go and do this.'

"So communication is really important, especially with a big family. Everybody gets assigned tasks that they are responsible for. The older kids do their own laundry, and it's an important skill, especially for the kids in high school, getting ready for college. The younger ones really have to put their own laundry away. Everybody has their jobs in the household. We're all part of a family, and then, me working on balancing my role as a mom, as a wife and as a business owner.

"I think with large families, you're not afraid to give your older children responsibilities and your younger kids responsibilities, as well, that are age-appropriate. You're just not afraid to do it because you just can't do it all. Being part of a family, we accomplish things together and we have disappointments together."

I've always seen that Alice's family is almost like a little community; it's a mini town that she is managing. Alice is the mayor. It's fabulous to watch in action.

Alice spoke to my assessment and admiration of how well her home runs, "It's a balancing act. It really is, and there are some days that I will say, 'Oh, my; I have a lot of mom friends who beat themselves up over the details. They feel, 'Oh, we didn't do this perfect.' 'I didn't handle this situation perfectly', and sometimes it comes down to accepting that I'm doing my best. The next time I will handle it a little bit more differently.

"It comes down to being happy and saying, 'The mom I want to be lets me work this many hours, so that's twenty hours or 40 hours', or for me, balancing maybe working at night when the little ones are in bed, because the big ones are all up watching TV. Or getting up in the morning to try to get some projects done and e-mails done, setting up a schedule, so I can balance having a meeting and then going to help out at a preschool party because that, to me, is important.

"I want to be there when they have that event going on at their schools. I try to find that balance, and even moms who decide to stay home full time need balance. I did that and kind of took a year off because I needed to figure out where I wanted to be, and I think that was very important for me. I needed to figure out that I can't burn the candle on both ends. I have to find out what works for me and how I'm wired.

"I took a year off to figure that out, because I knew I loved my job as a physical therapist. I love the boards that I serve on, I want to do a good job on the boards I serve; I don't want to just sit, I want to be active on boards and active in my kids' lives as well.

"Sometimes it's about, re-evaluating and then having a strong support system to do it. Kids need to know that, 'Hey, I appreciate my mom where she's at,' and sometimes we forget that, because you don't get that exactly from your kids. Most likely, they're not going to say that until they're 30 years old, out of the house, and have kiddos of their own."

I can honestly say, it has been a true blessing for me to have Alice Beckett-Rumberger in my life. When I keynoted the United Way Powerful Connections for Women Conference, I had tears in my eyes when I called her up to the stage.

She is my go-to friend. When Alice calls me up and says, "Hey, we need to get off this work roller coaster. Let's have a field trip for the day." We will take the kids to the Aviary to see the birds or to play at the pumpkin patch. Beyond that... Alice Beckett-Rumberger is a connector, a sounding board and a keeper of secrets over a glass of sangria while our children play.

Tania Grubbs:
Fairmont and Jazz at Andy's

I recall the first time I saw Tania Grubbs belt out a tune. I listened to her do a lovely set at the Fairmont Hotel. I liked her vibe and her music. When she pulled a very un-diva like move and passed me the mic to belt out Big Spender with her band, I knew she would be a life-long friend.

Tania explained her journey to performer, "My first CD 'Lost in the Stars,' was a huge accomplishment in my life. I learned a tremendous deal about myself, my worth, my shortcomings and about the music industry. It's just the beginning and I plan to do more in the future.

"I wasn't just doing it for myself. I was also modeling for my family, our children and other people. If you have a dream you desire, follow through with that dream and make it a reality.

"In my college days, I met a woman who was a professional, quite famous vocalist. She gave me some advice that I never forgot. She said, 'Be sure to have a life.' Oftentimes people are climbing a professional ladder and they forget about having a life during the climb. I'll never forget it.

"I have several role models, but they are mostly people I've never met, women who inspire me musically. There are a few singers in the region that I've developed a nice sisterhood with.

"I just discussed with my husband this past summer that I felt it was time for me to reach out to people I've admired, maybe take some workshops, and get to know some of these artists that I admire. I know they have had some of the same good and bad experiences that I have had. It would be interesting to get their perspective, hear their stories and share some music!

"I was born into a large family. Because of having so many different aged siblings, our house was a place where friends and family members would come and go. We always welcomed people in and celebrated who they were. I recall sharing conversations, laughs and tears… all of it.

"I am now a mother, and our family by design is quite different. We are a unit. My role as Tania, the mother/wife has been to protect, love and nurture them. Also, I must share what I know is true. I model what I am most proud of and share with an open heart. As a mother, I am loving and forgiving. I also think it is vital to proud of yourself.

"I am raising a child with unique needs; I'm not going to lie. There have been some really rough patches, especially when our child was younger, situations were often frustrating. Sometimes I would be afraid. There were days of anxiety and worry; I experienced all of it. I worry about my other children and how having a sibling with autism has affected their lives.

"Fortunately, when we gained the support of other families like us and we educated ourselves, we felt more empowered. We learned not to sweat the small stuff... even when others might consider it big stuff. You learn to build a thick exoskeleton.

"And please forgive for this, but you... learn to not to take anyone's shit. Sometimes it seems that everyone has something to say or advice to offer, but help usually isn't something that is given.

"Many mothers may feel that they may not be measuring up to what they see on their computers or TVs. I urge you to... Do what's right for you. Use social media as a positive tool, not to form judgments about yourself. As a vocalist, I am on social media for the performing that I do, and other musical events in which I am directly involved. When I use social media to get the word out about what I do, where I'm going to be or what I'm involved in next, it's really just information. I also use it to share special proud moments about our family, and milestones.

"I think you should get to know young people. Pay attention to what they are doing... it will help keep you inspired and young at heart!

"One of the major reasons that I got back into singing music was I needed a release. I often call my music, my 'therapy'. It has always been something I've enjoyed doing; I was decent at it. People always encouraged me to continue to do it, including my family.

"I hope I can inspire other moms. I would like them to be encouraged to try something new, revisit something that they love doing, and to not be afraid. Life does not stand still. Go get it!"

Chapter 10:

Serenity

The glorious scent of roses wafted through the air as I sat in my luxurious robe, soaking in the serene beauty of the Four Seasons spa. My mind was a peace and my soul was comforted as I sipped the jasmine tea and nibbled on the apricot. It is in moments of calm reflection that one can soak in tranquility.

What if you can't be at a high-end spa, today? What if the baby is screaming, your boss is sending frantic emails or you simply are having a rough day? How can you find inner serenity then?

Kimberly Wilson:

The Women's Center and Hip, Tranquil, Ventures

I sat in the Literary District of Paris, France as I interviewed Tranquility Du Jour expert, Kimberly Wilson. She had just hosted an incredible retreat, wherein I learned writing techniques and I did yoga with a wonderful group of lady authors. Penning in Paris was absolutely a profoundly, life-changing experience. Kimberly explained her journey of how she became known as the tranquil, hip chick through podcasts, books, retreats and even a fabulous yoga-inspired clothing line.

Kimberly took us on the journey, "It all began in Oklahoma. I moved to D.C. about twenty years ago. I was working in a law firm as a trademark paralegal, and I thought there has to be more to life. I was in my mid-twenties, looking forward to retirement. I knew that there had to be more out there.

"I read the book, *The Artist Way*, by Julia Cameron, really it's taken me on this profound journey of uncovering my own creativity. I opened a yoga studio, and began writing books and leading retreats. It's really just been a huge, opening experience that I credit to connecting to a source of creativity beyond a cubicle in a law firm."

Kimberly referred to some of the teachings that she did during the retreat in Paris, "One of the things that we talked about in the writing course this week is this idea of emulating those who you admire. When you are reading, whose words do you love? Similarly, who is it that you love their lifestyle? Maybe you see what they are doing and you say to yourself, 'I could do that. I could launch an Etsy store, I could lead a retreat in France, or I could write an e-book.' Just noticing what is their journey? What's taken them to where they are?

"It is a long journey of exploration and putting yourself out there. Really tap into what it is that feeds and nurtures your soul. Then see what's missing in the market, bringing that forth."

During our retreat, Kimberly and the ladies talked about eliminating things that no longer serve you in your lives. Kimberly explained, "That was a really big piece with regard to the lecture this week on finding your voice. I was reading from William Zinsser's book, *On Writing Well*, which is a classic. For anyone interested in developing writing skills, I highly recommend it. He talked about how as an artist, some of the hardest pieces, but the most profound, are figuring out what to eliminate from your project.

"We can be interested in so many things, and it doesn't mean you can't do them all, but sometimes when you're writing or you have a message that you're putting out there, you shouldn't bombard your audience with everything all at once. Instead, hone in on what you are drawn to; we need to eliminate from our lives in order to add more. For example, maybe try a little less TV and replacing it with writing time.

"Being authentic in ourselves and in our writing is really important. One of the things that William Zinsser says in that book that I recommended is that you shouldn't be afraid to imitate initially. Read the works of great masters who really get what it is you're trying to put out there; and whether that's a website, book or its artwork even if you're imitating to a degree, it's not going to be the same, because you bring your own life experience, your own personality, the whole shebang.

"With that, as you begin to emulate and see what really works for you, then you can begin to really hone in on what is your authentic voice. Many other artists will influence it.

"So being in Paris right now, there are so many things that are on my heart; like, I hope that you will eat rose petal ice cream and savor life.

"As Martha Graham talked about, it is important to put yourself there and share it with the world. If you don't, it is almost as if you are holding something back what the world needs. It could be profound and really help another person. So what is it that is your gift? What is it that you want to share? What is it is that you want to say? How is it that you have been touched? How has loss changed you, and how can you speak to that?

"Whatever it is; whether it's a class, website, book or artwork… the world needs to hear what you have to say. Get out there and let us know what's on your heart and live your best life."

Crystal Hayward:

Holistic Healing Enterprise

Crystal has a gentle way about her. Most of the times I have seen her in person, she has been dressed to the nines on a red carpet with me. She always has a kind word and she excels in the holistic field.

Crystal Hayward explained our connection, "Before I met Dr. Shellie, I heard so many fabulous things about her. Everyone was saying, 'You must meet Dr. Shellie', so I felt like I knew her long before we actually we met in person. In 2012, Shellie and I were introduced through Olga Maria (Dreams in Heels, Fashion PR) and Maggie Delaney (EPN, CEO) at The EPN Triple Launch Party in NYC. Both ladies are featured in this book series as well. Including Shellie, they are all powerful ladies who inspire me daily through their example.

"Medical doctors are prominent in my family. Both of my grandparents met and fell in love in Harbin, China while in medical school; my mother's sister, who we affectionately call "Fifi", raised me. She's in primary care and was an oncologist until she was diagnosed with breast cancer in 1997. She stopped administering chemo soon after because of her experience. Although I was exposed to 'traditional medicine', I always felt there had to be another way of treating those with illnesses. In some instances, prescription meds are necessary. I'm not carelessly ruling them out completely. I didn't go to medical school; I'm only trained as a hypnotherapist, which often works much better than traditional "talk therapy" aka psychotherapy.

"I call my business Holistic Healing Enterprise. I hope to collaborate with other healers who have the same passionate purpose to help others with compassion and empathy. Most of my work is spiritual, inward as I get to the root of where a trauma originates. The only way to heal is to come to terms with our past. Repressing our pain only magnifies it. Therefore, acknowledging where the wound originates, we can effectively heal.

"We work together as a team. I do not have patients. Instead, I have clients; they share deep things with me in total confidentiality. Just like any other any kind of connection, if you don't have trust then you cannot grow."

Crystal described her personal love story, "Paul and I met in October, 2012. We were guests at a Halloween yacht party (again, through Maggie Delany and her husband Hubert). According to Paul, seeing me was 'love-at-first-sight'. "As a single mom, it took me a bit longer to warm up. However, my feelings grew when I saw how Paul interacted with my daughter, Kylee who was then 2 1/2.

Neither of us was actively looking for love, so I suppose our relationship is destiny.

"In the short time we have been together, our relationship had been tested. Within our first year together, Paul was diagnosed with Level 3 brain cancer. After a lifesaving surgery, they removed a brain tumor that was the size of three golf balls. The following year, he had another brain surgery removing 90% of Paul's brain tumor with a chance of his becoming a paraplegic, suffering memory loss, and possibly death. The doctors gave us no other choice.

"Thank God, Paul survived the four-hour surgery. Afterwards, he had intense chemo & radiation treatments. We went through more in two years than some couples experience in a lifetime.

"I am proud to say that, today, Paul is a cancer survivor. The cherry on top was when he proposed to me after his second surgery. Of course, I said, 'Yes!'

"Empowering women is a huge passion of mine. Especially in the world we live in today, raising a daughter. I am blessed to have such a strong network of family and friends, mainly women who support my decisions. They are all amazing individuals who do not judge me. It is important for girls to grow up knowing they are loved, cherished and honored unconditionally simply for who they are.

"In some cultures, being a female is a burden. Despite the challenging circumstances in my life, I believe that a daughter is the world's most precious blessing. Boys are special too, but as a woman raising a daughter, I can definitely see myself in her eyes. Empowering women is priceless.

"Fathers can empower their daughters too. In fact, I know many men who identify themselves as 'feminists'. They are men who appreciate women who understand our struggle to balance career, family and time to cultivate ourselves. It is truly beautiful to know such individuals. I feel feminism has a negative stigma. All it means is honoring feminine energy: nurturing, compassion and creation."

Crystal explained ways that we can find serenity and calm, "I can center myself no matter who is around. I have an uncanny ability to zone everyone else out through meditation, no matter where I am. Knowing basic yoga positions helps. I just seek out a cozy corner where nobody can bother me. Anybody who is around me can see I'm in my sacred space.

"Serenity stems from within. I have some rituals I do to center myself and find inner peace. I start by going somewhere quite where I can lock the door. I have a large Jacuzzi bathtub in my home. I love essential oils in my bath water (especially lavender); it is very soothing to the senses and naturally releases tension in the muscles.

Sometimes I sit in silence. Other times I pray silently to myself and connect with the higher energy surrounding me. The Law of Attraction works best when you are at peace.

As a child, I always wanted to be a writer but never knew how it would happen. A few years ago, I was given an opportunity to tell my story and of course, I took it. The book is collaboration with 13 other women. Each of us has our own chapter. We are still going through the publishing process. In my chapter, I discuss the many hardships I experienced in childhood until my aunt and her husband adopted me in 1989. Since I was born, until I was 8 years old, I survived abuse, abandonment and a natural disaster. In my heart, there were times I wondered why I was born because of all the suffering I witnessed and experienced. Today, I am thankful for God's mercy. He was strengthening me. He knew that I would do great things with my life. In fact, I never complain when going through a life test. We are never given more than we can handle.

Sometimes we feel so small and even insignificant in the eyes of the world. Inspirational words that get me through hard times are by Margaret Mead who said, 'Never doubt that a small group of thoughtful, committed citizens can change the world; indeed, it's the only thing that ever has.'

"Ladies, there is a light at the end of the tunnel. Never give up on your aspirations. Stay strong. I am sending you all love and big healing hugs."

Dorit Brauer:
Live Your Best Life, LLC and
The Brauer Institute for Holistic Medicine

Dorit Brauer is the owner of the Brauer Institute for Holistic Medicine and author of the award-winning book *Girls Don't Ride Motorbikes – A Spiritual Adventure Into Life's Labyrinth*. Dorit explained that her book, "chronicles my modern day pilgrimage in which I embark onto a 7,430 mile solo motorcycle adventure across the US to walk labyrinths. On my journey, I recount poetic life stories spanning my youth on a dairy farm in Germany, a 10-week solo-backpacking trip in Brazil, the turmoil of living in Tel Aviv, to my most recent chronicles in the United States. As I traveled cross-country from labyrinth to labyrinth, these stories were woven together intricately to provide insights allowing the reader to reflect on their own spiritual journey.

"The title of the book, *Girls Don't Ride Motorbikes*, comes from a mantra of my youth, embedded into my mind by my father. Born from very traditional parents with their own expectations, I had the courage to make my own path. I pursued everything I wasn't supposed to and found adventure and true fulfillment in life.

"I am living my best life and intend to inspire everyone else to listen to their inner yearnings and follow the voice of their hearts.

"Labyrinths are sacred circles found in every culture around the globe, dating back thousands of years. The circle has no beginning and no end. It is a doorway to another dimension and it allows us to become whole and experience oneness, fulfilling the deepest yearning of the human soul. The sacred circle represents our origin and final destination, our divine essence that exists beyond time and space.

"The labyrinth is not to be confused with a maze, where you can take choices and reach dead ends. Mazes became popular during the period of rationalism in the 15th century, emphasizing reasoning and thinking. This was also a time when the holistic understanding of the universe lessened. The body, mind connection and the knowledge of how the mind rules matter vanished. It is interesting to notice that now we have come full circle. In the last 20 years, the labyrinth movement in the Unites States has flourished with dozens of new labyrinth created every year.

"The labyrinth is a spiritual transformation power tool that answers our call to wholeness. It allows you to reach states of clarity, during troubled times and turmoil. Its single winding path invites you to relax, give up control and trust.

"As you walk the labyrinth, consider the three R's. Release, Receive and Reflect. Following the journey into the labyrinth, contemplate releasing everything that does not serve your highest good. With every step, visualize breathing in bright shining healing light. You exhale all concerns, worries, painful memories, aches from your body, as well as beliefs and perceptions that do not resonate with the light. Enjoy this cleansing and purification process.

"The center of the labyrinth represents your connection to the divine, your higher self and it is a place of unity and oneness. Here you may ask for guidance to life's challenges. Be assured that the answers to your questions will emerge in the days following your labyrinth walk. Now as you have exhaled everything that does not serve you any longer, you may visualize breathing in the light and breathing it out; the light within you and all around you grows and expands. You become a vessel for the divine light; let your light shine bright and radiant.

"Then trace your steps back out of the labyrinth. Reflect on your journey, and count your blessings and all the good you have received throughout your life. Focus on gratitude, happy memories, moments of joy and love. Every thought that enters your mind creates reality. Reflect, choose your thoughts carefully and say thank you. Inner Peace and Serenity can be yours. Take the first step today. To find a labyrinth in your area, please check the World Wide Labyrinth Locator: www.labyrinthlocator.com.

"The regular practice of meditation and guided imagery is the most powerful form of preventative medicine. It reduces stress, which is a major cause of many diseases. Meditation and guided imagery shows you how to achieve positive changes in your body through the power of your mind.

"Every thought that enters your mind creates reality. On a personal level, you can very easily observe this fact. If you entertain positive thoughts and feel happy, you are having a good day. If you are down and upset, the opposite happens.

"I would like to share three simple meditation exercises with you:

1. Breathe to your abdomen. When you are stressed, you breathe to your chest. Abdominal breathing activates your parasympathetic nervous system and breaks the stress cycle.

2. Focus on happy memories. Feel the vibration of happiness and joy. Feel the smile on your lips. Research has shown that a happy outlook on life, strengthens your immune system and please remember that whatever you focus on, you get more of.

3. Visualize yourself surrounded by bright-shining, benevolent light. The light is all around you. It protects you and shields you from all harmful influences. Through your breathing, you bring this light into your body.

"Let the peace fill you entirely and exhale everything

that does not serve your highest good. The light cleanses and purifies your entire being. Make this a daily habit, so you don't internalize negative emotions and stress, that over time, may manifest as disease in your physical body.

"Scientific studies have proven that the regular practice of meditation and guided imagery has many positive benefits. These include: control of blood pressure with less medication, reduction in chronic pain, improvements in sleep, reduction of premenstrual symptoms, and reduction in anxiety.

"Please enjoy the free meditation video 'Heal yourself & Heal the World' at www.doritbrauer.com. You are invited to practice this meditation daily and experience a healthy, happy and relaxed life."

Women, always follow your heart. Grow in your connections and love.

About the Author:
Dr. Shellie Hipsky

Dr. Shellie Hipsky (www.ShellieHipsky.com) inspires, educates, and entertains internationally. For over a decade, she served as a professor at Robert Morris University and was honored by FacultyRow.com as a "Super Professor" chosen from over 100,000 professors globally.

Dr. Shellie Hipsky inspired internationally with her personal life story and the stories of the amazing people in her book *Ordinary People Extraordinary Planet*. She recently co-authored the international best seller *The Missing Piece in the Law of Attraction*. She has published hundreds of articles and her other book titles include: *Drama Discovery, Arts Alive, Differentiated Literacy and Language Arts for the Elementary Classroom, and Mentoring Magic: Pick the Card for Your Success.*

Hipsky was the Executive Producer and TV Talk show Host of "Inspiring Lives with Dr. Shellie" which was taped in an NBC studio and viewed around the world. She was deemed "Inspirational Woman of the Month" in *Inspirational Woman Magazine* and a "Luminary Author" for *Inspire Me Today.* She earned the Women's Small Business Association's "Best Business Woman" of the Year in Pittsburgh in 2013, in Washington, D.C. she earned the 2015 "Entrepreneur of the Year in Inspiration and Empowerment", and the National Association for Professional Women's "VIP Woman of the Year" in 2015.

A performer and volunteer since she was a child, she is renowned locally for her acting/singing talents and utilizes them to host galas such as the Fabulous Forties which have raised over $100,000 for homeless children in shelters. Active on multiple non-profit boards, she is extremely passionate about the Homeless Children's Education Fund charity and serves on the advisory board. Dr. Shellie has been invited to present at international conferences, at Oxford University in England, and spoke to over a thousand people at Pepperdine University and keynoted the United Way Professional Connections for Women Conference.

The latest of her 8 published books: the *Common Threads* trilogy provides *Inspiration, Empowerment,* and *Balance* based on 100 amazing interviews for Empowering Women Radio!